frosch

*richard strauss
die frau ohne schatten*

*critical discography
compiled by
john hunt*

*"fr-o-sch"(frosch meaning frog) was the endearing
acronym coined by the composer and his librettist
hofmannsthal during the opera's gestation period*

Frosch

Discography of the Richard Strauss Opera Die Frau ohne Schatten

John Hunt

© John Hunt 2012

ISBN 978-1-901395-27-3

Travis & Emery Music Bookshop
17 Cecil Court
London
WC2N 4EZ
United Kingdom.
Tel. (+44) (0) 20 7240 2129.
newpublications@travis-and-emery.com

contents

bibliography/*page 6*

introduction/*page 7*

the conductors/*page 13*

synopsis and characters/*page 15*

supporting roles/*page 25*

orchestral fantasy/*page 25*

summary of the performances/*page 28*

the performances/*page 30*

appendix a: performances not heard/*page 202*

appendix b: officially published excerpts/*page 206*

list of discography subscribers/*page 210*

6
bibliography

richard strauss: chronik zu leben und werk
herausgegeben von florian trenner
published by verlag dr. richard strauss 2003

chronik der wiener staatsoper 1869-2009
zusammengestellt von andreas und oliver lang
published by wiener staatsoper 2009

maurus pacher: ohne kostüm und maske
(die andere operngeschichte)
published by ullstein verlag 1991

and programme books of the royal opera, welsh national opera, edinburgh international festival, sadlers wells theatre, wiener staatsoper, bayerische staatsoper, deutsche oper berlin, salzburger festspiele, sächsische staatsoper dresden and niedersächsisches staatstheater hannover

introduction

"Die Frau ohne Schatten" was Hugo von Hofmannsthal's conscious endeavour to create the great German opera: the one Goethe always dreamed of but could never find the composer for. Hofmannsthal found his composer. Visionary and pragmatist met."
- Andrew Porter

The idea of a discography devoted to a single piece of musical literature is not new, and of course for much repertoire that has been repeatedly recorded over the past eighty years or more, there is a pressing need to catalogue and evaluate the wealth of versions available to a modern listener.

The case of the Richard Strauss opera *Die Frau ohne Schatten (The Woman without a Shadow)* is somewhat special. Starting with the enterprising Decca recording of 1955, there have been no more than half a dozen officially sanctioned issues of the work: two of those have been taken direct from stage performances, two others linked to concurrent stage presentations, leaving another two which can be described as studio recordings in the traditional sense. What need therefore for a discographic traversal of such a small field?

My passion for *Die Frau ohne Schatten*, fanned in no small measure by the enthusiasm of other collectors (notably Neville Sumpter), has led to us amassing an incredible number of extant radio transmissions and in-house recordings of the piece. The term "in-house" can refer to both professional quality recordings made for the archive by the theatre where the opera performance is taking place, as well as private tapings made by audience members which of course will vary greatly in terms of sound quality. Thanks to the medium of Compact Disc and its associated technology, many of the recordings are circulating in sufficient quality to be heard with pleasure, and to be evaluated alongside the so-called "official" editions.

A new type of discography calls for a new layout, and I have devoted a double-page spread to each version of the opera. The right-hand page gives recording venue and dates, names of orchestra, chorus and conductor, catalogue numbers (where they apply) and finally comments upon the particular recording: these comments are, it must be emphasised, personal and subjective, and are intended only as a guide for the listener. The preceding left-hand page is devoted to a list of the principal soloists needed for this epic (six major roles and a further seven important supporting parts). In the majority of the recordings, voices for the further minor characters (such as night watchmen, unborn children or servants) are taken either by unnamed chorus members or duplicated by singers of the seven supporting parts.

My original plan had been also to include timings for each of the three acts (Strauss conveniently composed each act to be approximately of an hour's duration, in other words the perfect fit for a single compact disc). But there are so many tempo variations between performances as well as a variety of cuts in the score which were at different items officially sanctioned by the composer, as to render timings to be of little real value. And on the subject of those cuts, I think that we must accept the composer's practical wishes: the only instance where any real structural damage is done by cutting is in the opera's concluding ensemble, which, when one hears it complete, makes a glorious close to the piece.

As to the order in which the recordings are listed, I have decided against chronology in favour of a grouping around each of the principal operatic centres which has taken on the daunting task of performing the work, starting with Vienna, the stage which gave its premiere: the very first Viennese recording survives in fragments only, but because of its historical importance is placed at the top of the list.

The question often asked about those first performances of the opera is: why not Dresden? The Saxon capital had, after all, facilitated and then witnessed the triumphs of *Salome*, *Elektra* and *Der Rosenkavalier*. Or on the other hand, why not Salzburg, where Strauss and Hofmannsthal formed two parts of the triumvirate which was about to inaugurate the first Salzburg Festival (presumably the lack of a suitable theatre building to house the ambitious scenario gives us the answer to that question). And so the world premiere fell to the Wiener Staatsoper, which at the time was most anxious to bind Strauss as its music director.

Appendices at the end of the discography list both additional versions which I have not been able to hear, and also the comparatively small number of separately published extracts.

My thanks for assistance goes on this occasion to John Hancock, Klaus Heinze, Roderick Krüsemann, Tim Lockley, the late Elsa Mayer-Lismann, Neville Sumpter and several collectors who have supplied copies of tapes but who wish to remain anonymous. Several of the private CD labels listed are produced by these collectors, whose contact details can easily be ascertained by anyone with the basic skill to search the internet.

10

Considering the importance which the composer Richard Strauss would come to occupy in my own operatic pantheon, I was really quite a slow beginner in my exploration of his stage works. By the early 1960s I had encountered only *Der Rosenkavlier* in London, Salzburg and Würzburg, *Arabella* in Salzburg and Düsseldorf, *Die schweigsame Frau* in Salzburg and London and both *Elektra* and *Ariadne auf Naxos* in Salzburg. Indeed, it was fascinating to read at that time that of the composer's fifteen stage works (a figure that does not include ballet or incidental music), five of them had not yet been performed in Britain at all. What a major lapse, I thought, for a composer who in my view represented all that was best in German opera.

I was lucky enough to be present when the first of those five missing works finally revealed itself to a British audience in 1966. *Die Frau ohne Schatten*, which I would best describe as a fairy tale on an epic scale and whose only antecedent would be Mozart's *Die Zauberflöte*, was presented in the cramping confines of the old Sadler's Wells Theatre by the visiting company of the Hamburgische Staatsoper (a few years earlier, that very same company had performed a similar feat in the same theatre by bringing Wieland Wagner's own production of *Lohengrin* to London, with the magnificent Astrid Varnay bringing the unsuspecting Sadler's Wells audience to its feet with Ortrud's malevolent Act Two outburst).

The 1966 performance of *Die Frau ohne Schatten* was for me the beginning of an exploratory journey through this fascinating work which continues to the present day, and it was followed up only a year later when the enterprising Georg Solti presented the opera for the first time at Covent Garden. The twelve performances of that production which I attended in the course of the next nine years formed the basis of my getting to know the serious yet multifarious piece.

Very much earlier, when conductor Clemens Krauss had brought the *Frau* to the Salzburg Festival in 1933, he had invited an old friend from his days at the Frankfurt Opera to come and give an introductory lecture on a piece still considered extremely difficult for the average opera-goer. This was Mita Mayer-Lismann, whose daughter Elsa was to come to Britain as a Jewish refugee and, after the Second World War, gained a reputation as an enthusiastic lecturer on opera as well as eventually founding a workshop training young singers in stagecraft. When I first met Elsa, herself a trained pianist and singer, she was giving introductory talks on the operas being played each year at the Glyndebourne Festival, and when Welsh National Opera brought their production of the *Frau* to London in 1981, she presented an evening of fascinating insights into the piece. Elsa's animated descriptions of the characters and situations remain with me to this day, and I am sure that they played a part in maintaining my own obsession with this opera.

Having already referred several times to the fact that this particular opera can seem dauntingly esoteric to the new listener, I cannot emphasise too much my conviction that familiarising onesef with libretto and the development of the principal characters will easily overcome initial difficulty. The process is much abettted by the potent music offered by Richard Strauss, with its heady mix of Wagnerian grandeur and deeply moving lyricism. The synopsis which I reproduce is based on the original scenario of the librettist Hugo von Hofmannsthal, as are the ensuing brief character sketches (to these I have also added my personal recommendations, based on the recorded evidence, as to which singers offer the most penetrating interpretations of their roles).

12

It cannot be stressed sufficiently that for the purposes of this study, even those recordings of the opera which exist in video form have been auditioned in sound only, reflecting my intense distrust in the unwanted directorial glosses now being inflicted on us on a regular basis. Although the critical fraternity is nowadays inclined to scoff at any opera production which is not accompanied by a "concept", I have yet to meet any member of the paying public who is even remotely enthusiastic about such intrusions!

John Hunt 2012

13
the conductors recorded
numbers refer to the performance number, and are not page numbers; names in bold type are the compiler's personal preference for finest achievement

marc albrecht	18	68						
richard armstrong	64							
michael boder	19	20						
karl böhm	2	3	4	5	8	9	10	31
	72	73	75	76	77	78		
anthony bramall	49							
andrew davis	86							
christoph von dohnanyi	11	40	41	43	54	57	65	84
bernard haitink	66							
heinrich hollreiser	33	34						
marek janowski	79	82						
herbert von karajan	6	7						
joseph keilberth	22							
rudolf kempe	21							
berislav klobucar	80							
clemens krauss	1							
gustav kuhn	60							
erich leinsdorf	81							
ferdinand leitner	38	71	74					
leopold ludwig	70							
michael luig	45							
zubin mehta	53							
friedrich pleyer	58							
christof prick	83							
john pritchard	42							
wolfgang sawallisch	23	24	25	26	27	28	29	50
peter schneider	30							
giuseppe sinopoli	14	15	17	51	52			
stefan soltesz	46							

14
the conductors recorded/concluded
georg solti	12	13	62	63
horst stein	56			
pinchas steinberg	59			
otmar suitner	32			
muhai tang	69			
christian thielemann	16	35	36	85
edo de waart	67			
erich wächter	44			
heinz wallberg	39			
sebastian weigle	47			
ralf weikert	55			
franz welser-möst	61			
simone young	48			
winfried zillig	37			

synopsis and characters
Act One

The emperor of a far-eastern island kingdom is married to the daughter of the fairy king Keikobad. He won his wife while hunting: a white gazelle he was pursuing had suddenly turned into a beautiful young woman. Now, as the emperor's wife, she has lost the gift of being able to turn herself back into her animal form. But she is not fully human either: she cannot cast a shadow, because she has not given birth to a child. If this is not remedied within a year, according to the law of the spirit world she must return to her father and the emperor will be turned to stone.

A messenger sent by Keikobad announces to the nurse, a servant of the spirit realm who has followed the empress, that her mistress has three days left to obtain a shadow. The emperor's red falcon, who helped to hunt down the gazelle and knows what has been decreed, also warns that the emperor will be turned to stone. The empress implores the nurse to find her a shadow. For the nurse, the only solution is to obtain one from another woman. The two women take advantage of the fact that the emperor is away hunting for three days to visit the human world.

The dyer Barak lives and works in a miserable hut with his young wife and three parasitic brothers. The nurse and empress wait until the dyer has gone out before they enter in disguise. By conjuring up fabulous illusions of wealth and happiness, the nurse tries to convince the dyer's wife, who is dissatisfied with her miserable existence, to sell her shadow. Although distrustful at first, she finally agrees to take on the two women as servants. On returning home, Barak is perplexed by his wife's strange behaviour but, confident of a better future, he accepts the new situation.

Act Two

In order to deepen the rift between the dyer and his wife, the nurse takes advantage of the husband's absence to conjure up the apparition of a handsome young man. The wife, however, is able to resist the temptation. On his return from the market, Barak generously hands out food to his brothers and a crowd of begging children. The wife turns away in disgust and heaps scorn on her husband.

The red falcon has guided the emperor to the falconer's house, where the empress has told her husband she intends to spend three days. The emperor observes his wife creeping secretly into the house with the nurse. In a fit of jealous rage he wants to kill her, but cannot bring himself to do so and flees in despair.

The next day the nurse and dyer's wife are waiting impatiently for Barak to leave the hut. When he asks for something to drink, the nurse gives him a sleeping potion. Once again she conjures up the apparition of the young man to tempt the dyer's wife; a touch of his ghostly hand, however, makes her tremble in fright and she wakes her husband. Barak cannot understand why his wife is upset. She leaves the house together with the nurse, while the empress, in her role as a humble servant, remains behind with the confused dyer..

Back in the falconer's house, the empress is tormented by bad dreams. She feels guilty towards Barak. Then she sees the emperor entering a strange room. Awaking from the dream in fright, she realises that she is responsible for bringing disaster on both the emperor and Barak

In order to test her husband once again, his wife falsely accuses herself of adultery and admits to having sold her shadow in return for eternal youth. In so doing she renounces the chance of having children. Barak is aghast and wants to kill his wife. As if by magic a sword appears in his hand. In this instant she sees her husband for the first time in his full human measure. She retracts her false confession and is prepared to die by his hand. Suddenly the earth opens and the couple is swallowed up. The empress, who did not seize the wife's shadow, is brought to safety by the nurse.

Act Three
Deep beneath the earth the dyer and his wife are lying in separate vaults. Both admit to being at fault and finally a voice from above tells them to ascend.

A boat brings the nurse and empress to Keikobad's spirit kingdom. Against the nurse's will, the empress resolves to submit herself to her father's test in order to save the emperor. She disassociates herself from the nurse, who is henceforth condemned to live amongst the human beings she hates.

Keikobad's guardian of the threshold entices the empress to drink from the water of life in order to finally obtain the shadow and save the emperor. But she is not prepared to sacrifice the happiness of Barak and his wife to save her own husband, now turned to stone – she would rather die together with him. By this act of overcoming her fear, she frees the emperor and gains the shadow she has longed for.

Barak and his wife are also reconciled. She has regained her own shadow which becomes the bridge over the abyss separating them. Voices of the unborn who are about to attain life join in the jubilation of the two couples.

kaiserin / the empress (soprano voice)

"Of the three-fold nature of the Kaiserin — part animal, part human, part spirit — only the animal and spirit aspects are apparent at the outset: these two together make her the strange being she is. In between, there is a vacuum — the humanity is missing. To acquire this humanity — that is the meaning of the whole work"..

In listing the recorded singers of each role, numbers refer to the performance number, and are not page numbers; names in bold type are the compiler's personal preferences for the most penetrating interpretation of that role

marion ammann	69			
susan anthony	19	46		
hildegard behrens	54			
ingrid bjoner	22	23	71	74
kirsten blanck	49			
silvana dussmann	47			
luana devol	29	57		
trude eipperle	38			
anne evans	64			
ruth falcon	65			
gabriele fontana	68			
catherine foster	20			
mechthild gessendorf	24			
amanda halgrimson	18			
heather harper	63			
sabine hass	25	34		
hildegard hillebrecht	31	62		
marilyn howell	45			
gundula janowitz	6			
mary jane johnson	84			
gwyneth jones	55			
hilde konetzni	2			
annelies kupper	37			
annemarie leber	39			

emily magee	48	61				
alessandra marc	35	51	67			
eva marton	40	41	50	79	81	82
johanna meier	83					
ricarda merbeth	59					
inga nielsen	30	52				
monica pick-hieronimi	44					
adrienne pieczonka	53					
leonie rysanek	4	5	7	8	9	10
	11	21	33	43	70	72
	73	75	76	77	78	80
anne schwanewilms	16					
ellen shade	56					
eleanor steber	3					
cheryl studer	13	26	27	28		
enriquetta tarres	32					
anna tomova-sintow	58	66				
viorica ursuleac	1					
sylvie valayre	36					
julia varady	12					
deborah voigt	14	15	17	85	86	
siw wennberg	42					
eva maria westbroek	60					

färberin/ the dyer's wife (dramatic soprano voice)

"A bizarre woman with a very beautiful soul: strange, moody, domineering and yet at the same time likeable".

janice baird	59	61		
hildegard behrens	12			
ingrid bjoner	24	25		
inge borkh	22	28	62	76
christine brewer	60	86		
elizabeth connell	47			
helga dernesch	63			
luana devol	18	35	46	52

20

ludmilla dvorakova	32				
lisa gasteen	48				
christel goltz	3	4	5		
janet hardy	45				
sabine hass	17	51	57		
evelyn herlitzius	16	20	68		
gwyneth jones	11	27	42	43	54
	55	58	65	66	84
maria kinas	38				
gladys kuchta	6	31	71		
christa ludwig	7	8	72	73	75
janis martin	29	34	83		
eva marton	13				
daniza mastilovic	74				
johanna meier	67				
birgit nilsson	10	23	40	41	79
	80				
elena pankratova	53				
deborah polaski	30	56			
brenda roberts	44				
marianne schech	21	70			
erna schlüter	37				
gabriele schnaut	14	15	19	36	85
ursula schröder-feinen	9	77	78		
else schulz	2				
liane synek	39				
kirsi tilhonen	69				
pauline tinsley	64				
ute vinzing	26	33			
caroline whisnant	49				
marilyn zschau	50	82			

amme/ the nurse (dramatic mezzo-soprano voice)
*"Her irridescent nature hovers between the demonic and the grotesque....
she knows the world of man with a penetrating and loveless knowledge"*

lilian bennigsen	21					
lioba braun	53					
irene dalis	70	72	73	75	76	
helga dernesch	24	28	42	43	65	83
mignon dunn	54	78	81	82		
wilja ernst-masuraitis	49					
diana eustrati	37					
brigitte fassbänder	27	50				
res fischer	38					
jane henschel	15	35	46	60	66	
ruth hesse	8	9	10	11	31	33
	34	36	40	41	63	77
	79	80				
grace hoffman	6	7	71	74		
elisabeth höngen	2	3	4	5		
julia juon	47	69				
sigrid kehl	32					
marjana lipovsek	13	14	29	30		
michaela martens	86					
krystina michalowska	44					
martha mödl	22	39				
donna morein	45					
patricia payne	64					
birgit remmert	61					
regina resnik	62					
gertrud rünger	1					
reinhild runkel	12	51	52	55	56	58
	67	85				
gabriele schnaut	48					
michaela schuster	16					
hanna schwarz	17	18	26			
anja silja	57	84				
doris soffel	20	59	68			
ildiko szönyi	19					
ute trekel-burkhardt	25					
astrid varnay	23					

kaiser/ the emperor (tenor voice)

"Of the five main characters, the Emperor is the least prominent. His fairytale fate – of being turned to stone and then redeemed again – is his most striking feature. His traits are typical rather than individual: he is the hunter and the lover".

heinrich bensing	37				
johan botha	14				
gerd brenneis	33	34	81		
ronald carter	45				
jean cox	44				
robert dean smith	59	86			
placido domingo	12				
jeffrey dowd	46				
sebastian feiersinger	71				
paul frey	66				
reiner goldberg	18	19	20		
stephen gould	16				
ben heppner	15	17			
horst hoffmann	58				
hans hopf	4	5	21		
robert ilosfalvy	42				
william johns	50	82	84		
matti kastu	64	77			
torsten kerl	53				
james king	8	9	10	11	23
	25	31	41	62	63
	67	72	73	78	80
waldemar kmentt	74				
rene kollo	26	40	54		
gary lakes	51				
karl liebl	39				
thomas moser	13	35	36	56	57
	85				
robert nagy	75	76			
ticho parly	70				

23

torsten ralf	2				
martin ritzmann	32				
lance ryan	49				
roberto sacca	61				
robert schunk	24	27	28	43	65
	83				
peter seiffert	29				
stuart skelton	47	48			
set svanholm	3				
jess thomas	6	7	22	79	
john treleavan	69				
jon villars	60				
klaus florian vogt	68				
franz völker	1				
jon frederic west	52				
wolfgang windgassen	38				
hermann winkler	55				
alan woodrow	30				

barak der färber/ the dyer (bass-baritone voice)

"Barak is no longer young, but he works as hard as anyone and is as strong as a camel. He earns the wherewithal to keep a young, pretty and dissatisfied wife, as well as his three disabled brothers".

theo adam	24	25			
norman bailey	64				
walter berry	7	8	9	10	11
	42	63	72	73	75
	76	77	78		
wolfgang brendel	30	35	85		
james courtney	83				
jose van dam	12				
michael dean	45				
albert dohmen	53				
gerd feldhoff	31	33	34	55	80
dietrich fischer-dieskau	22	23			

24

herbert grabe	39				
franz grundheber	17	18	20	41	54
	66	67			
robert hale	13				
franz hawlata	60	86			
josef herrmann	2				
marcus jupither	49				
karl kamann	3				
wolfgang koch	16				
karl kronenberg	37				
jean-philippe lafont	57	58			
donald mcintyre	40	62	74		
josef metternich	21				
alfred muff	26	28	50	84	
franz ferdinand nentwig	43	81			
siegmund nimsgern	65	79	82		
anthony raffell	44				
jukka rasilainen	19	69			
wilhelm schirp	38				
paul schöffler	5	70			
wolfgang schöne	36	46	56		
andrew schroeder	59				
terje stensvold	47	68			
falk struckmann	14	15			
daniel sumegi	48				
antonin svorc	32				
alan titus	29	51	52		
michael volle	61				
ludwig weber	4				
bernd weikl	27				
otto wiener	6				
mino yahia	71				

the supporting roles

geisterbote/spirit messenger (baritone voice)
stimme des falken/voice of the falcon (soprano voice)
erscheinung eines jünglings/apparition of a youth (tenor voice)
hüter der schwelle/guardian of the threshold (soprano voice)
stimme von oben/voice from above (contralto voice)

barak's three brothers
der einäugige/the one-eyed (bass voice)
der einarmige/the one-armed (bass voice)
der bucklige/the hunchback (tenor voice)

drei wächter/three nightwatchmen
stimmen der ungeborenen/voices of unborn children
dienerinnen/servant women
bettelkinder/beggar children
geisterstimmen/spirit voices

the orchestral fantasy
In the grim conditions of the 1940s the prospect of reviving Die Frau ohne Schatten must have seemed remote to the despondent composer, prompting him to arrange a symphonic suite of themes from the opera: this was completed in May 1946 and first played under conductor Karl Böhm in Vienna in June 1947. The opportunity to fashion a synthesis of the opera's orchestral interludes, in the manner of those made for Pelleas et Melisande and Peter Grimes, was missed, but conductor Erich Leinsdorf later produced his own version which comes closer to that idea. Two of the recordings listed overleaf are of Leinsdorf's realisation.

26
sinfonische fantasie (1946)
philadelphia orchestra
eugene ormandy
recorded on 14 april 1957 in the town hall philadelphia
lp: american columbia ML 5333/philips A01421L

staatskapelle berlin
otmar suitner
recorded on 15 july 1970 in the funkhaus nalepastrasse berlin-ost
lp: eterna 827 407/deutsche schallplatten (japan) ET 3005
cd: berlin classics 02442/90262/94722

detroit symphony orchestra
antal dorati
recorded between 14-16 november 1983 in the united artists auditorium detroit
lp: decca 411 8931
cd: decca 411 8932/444 3442

sächsische staatskapelle dresden
hans vonk
recorded at a concert on 26-27 may 1988 in the kulturpalast dresden
unpublished radio broadcast
mitteldeutscher rundfunk

rotterdams philharmonisch orkest
jeffrey tate
recorded in november 1991 in de doelen rotterdam
cd: emi 754 5812/575 6342

chicago symphony orchestra
daniel barenboim
recorded between 15 september-3 october 1992 in orchestra hall chicago
cd: erato 2292 459972

sächsische staatskapelle dresden
giuseppe sinopoli
recorded in may 1995 in the lukaskirche dresden
cd: deutsche grammophon 449 2162

nederlands philharmonisch orkest
hartmut haenchen
recorded at a concert in november 1996 in the concertgebouw amsterdam
cd: nederlands philharmonisch orkest NEDPHO 1020/
laserlight 18002

seattle symphony orchestra
gerard schwarz
recorded in 1998 in seattle
cd: delos 3109

wiener philharmoniker
christian thielemann
recorded at concerts in september 2002 in the musikvereinssaal wien
cd: deutsche grammophon 474 1922

buffalo philharmonic orchestra
joann falletta
recorded on 31 march-1 april 2008 in the kleinhaus music hall buffalo
cd: naxos 8.572041

deutsches sinfonieorchester berlin
peter ruzicka
recorded on 18 january 2010 in berlin
unpublished radio broadcast
radio brandenburg

symphonic interludes (arranged by erich leinsdorf)
philharmonia orchestra
erich leinsdorf
recorded between 14-16 september 1960 in the kingsway hall london
lp: capitol P 8548/SP 8548
cd: emi 565 6132

minnesota orchestra
kazushi oue
recorded at concerts in 1997 in minneapolis
cd: reference recordings RRCD 83

summary of the performances

vienna and salzburg/*performance numbers 1-16*
1 june 1933　　　　　　　　23 november 1943
11 june 1953　　　　　　　　9 november 1955
29 november-10 december 1955
8 june 1964　　　　　　　　11 june 1964
16 august 1974　　　　　　26 july 1975
23 october 1977　　　　　　6 november 1984
march-september 1989　　　july 1992
11 december 1999　　　　　6 may 2000
29 july 2011

dresden/*performance numbers 17-20*
november-december 1996　　5 september 2001
18 september 2004　　　　　26 march 2008

munich/*performance numbers 21-30*
31 august 1954　　　　　　21 november 1963
29 september 1976　　　　28 december 1981
21 november 1984　　　　　february-november 1987
12 july 1988　　　　　　　16 july 1988
8-11 november 1992　　　　30 september 2000

berlin/*performance numbers 31-36*
9 june 1964　　　　　　　21 march 1971
25 february 1981　　　　　11 may 1986
20 november 1999　　　　　28 december 2003

rest of germany/*performance numbers 37-49*
1950　　　　　　　　　　　11 september 1954
1 may 1964　　　　　　　　2 october 1977
8 january 1980　　　　　　16 march 1980
26 december 1983　　　　　1 may 1987
2 january 1994　　　　　　9 december 2001
17 february 2005　　　　　21 february 2007
27 october 2007

italy/*performance numbers 50-53*

6 march 1986	23 march 1996
14 april 1999	29 april 2010

france and switzerland/*performance numbers 54-61*

22 september 1980	24 november 1985
8 november 1992	20 march 1994
22 october 1995	6 october 2006
3 february 2008	19 december 2009

london/*performance numbers 62-66*

17 june 1967	5 april 1976
14 march 1981	30 june 1987
23 november 1992	

amsterdam/*performance numbers 67-68*

9 june 1990	20 september 2008

helsinki/*performance number 69*

6 february 2006

north and south america/*performance numbers 70-86*

24 september 1960	10 october 1965
17 december 1966	8 march 1969
13 october 1970	16 january 1971
11 february 1971	15 october 1976
1 april 1978	14 october 1979
30 september 1980	23 october 1981
19 november 1984	9 december 1989
10 december 1989	5 january 2002
30 november 2007	

performance no 1

kaiserin	**viorica ursuleac**
färberin	rose pauly
amme	**gertrud rünger**
kaiser	**franz völker**
barak	josef von manowarda
geisterbote	karl ettl
stimme des falken	eva hadrabova
erscheinung eines jünglings	georg maikl
hüter der schwelle	eva hadrabova
stimme von oben	enid szantho
der einäugige	viktor madin
der einarmige	alfred muzzarelli
der bucklige	william wernigk

only the singers whose names appear in bold type are heard in the surviving recorded excerpts from this performance

31

performance no 1

date 1 june 1933/public performance

venue staatsoper wien

orchestra orchester der wiener staatsoper

choirs chor der wiener staatsoper

conductor **clemens krauss**

catalogue numbers lp: ed smith UORC 345
lp: teletheater 120.747 (b)
cd: koch 3-1466-2 (a, b, c)
a) bleib und wache bis sie dich ruft
b) wenn das herz aus kristall
c) sind das die cherubin?
d) falke du wiedergefundener

comments

These precious fragments afford us a glimpse of a Viennese performance taking place only fourteen years after the work's world premiere in that very same theatre. They are among the earliest examples taken down on wax or decelith sheets by Hermann May with the authorisation of Staatsoper director Clemens Krauss.

It is clear from the manner in which Franz Völker delivers the lines of the Kaiser that a Siegmund or Parsifal type voice (and not necessarily that of a Siegfried) was needed to do justice to this major tenor part, in itself a rarity in the operas of Richard Strauss.

performance no 2

kaiserin	**hilde konetzni**
färberin	**else schulz**
amme	**elisabeth höngen**
kaiser	**torsten ralf**
barak	**josef herrmann**
geisterbote	**herbert alsen**
stimme des falken	**else böttcher**
erscheinung eines jünglings	**wenko wenkoff**
hüter der schwelle	**emmy loose**
stimme von oben	**melanie frutschnigg**
der einäugige	**georg monthy**
der einarmige	**marjan rus**
der bucklige	**william wernigk**

performance no 2

date	23 november 1943/public performance
venue	staatsoper wien
orchestra	orchester der wiener staatsoper
choirs	chor der wiener staatsoper
conductor	**karl böhm**
catalogue numbers	lp: ed smith UORC 345 cd: koch 3-1455-2/3-1460-2 *UORC 345 was a 2-lp set which also contained the fragments from 1933; 3-1460-2 contained only the scene vater bist du's?*

comments

Having already given the Frau in his Dresden period, Böhm was quick to revive the opera in Vienna when he took over the directorship in 1942. These extensive extracts, recorded backstage by engineer Hermann May, can because of their importance be treated under the heading of complete performances.

Ralf, Herrmann and Höngen had been brought to Vienna by Böhm from his Dresden company, whilst the other two female leads were taken with authority from Vienna forces: Schulz was a noted Salome who had sung that part under the composer's own direction.

The cast had no weaknesses, and Böhm gives majesty and power to what we hear of the orchestral interludes.

According to Gottfried Kraus, fragments were also recorded by May at the dress rehearsal a week earlier on 16 November.

performance no 3

kaiserin	**eleanor steber**
färberin	**christel goltz**
amme	**elisabeth höngen**
kaiser	**set svanholm**
barak	**karl kamann**
geisterbote	**otto wiener**
stimme des falken	**ilona steingruber**
hüter der schwelle	**ilona steingruber**

performance no 3

date	11 june 1953/public performance
venue	konzerthaus wien
orchestra	wiener philharmoniker
choirs	konzertvereingung wiener staatsopernchor
conductor	**karl böhm**
catalogue numbers	cd: golden melodram GM 60006/vai audio VAIA 1012/premiere opera 956 *vai audio edition contained only acts two and three which were incorrectly dated 4 june and incorrectly described as performed in munich*

comments

This was a heavily abbreviated concert performance, presented jointly by the Wiener Staatsoper and Ravag radio as part of the 1953 Wiener Festwochen.

Alongside the Kaiserin of American Eleanor Steber (whose other Strauss roles were Sophie, Marschallin, Ariadne and Arabella), Böhm also brought stalwarts from his Dresden and war-time Vienna ensembles.

Sadly the complete concert as issued by Golden Melodram is in inadequate sound quality, whereas the parts issued by VAI Audio are much more pleasant to listen to: presumably an Austrian Radio tape survives, which, if published, would give this item a much more important place in the Frau discography.

performance no 4

kaiserin	**leonie rysanek**
färberin	**christel goltz**
amme	**elisabeth höngen**
kaiser	**hans hopf**
barak	**ludwig weber**
geisterbote	**kurt böhme**
stimme des falken	**judith hellwig**
erscheinung eines jünglings	**karl terkal**
hüter der schwelle	**emmy loose**
stimme von oben	**hilde rössl-majdan**
der einäugige	**harald pröglhöf**
der einarmige	**oskar czerwenka**
der bucklige	**murray dickie**

performance no 4

date	9 november 1955/public peformance
venue	staatsoper wien
orchestra	orchester der wiener staatsoper
choirs	chor der wiener staatsoper
conductor	**karl böhm**
catalogue numbers	cd: orfeo C668 053D/premiere opera 2057 *excerpts from the recording also on rca/bmg 74321 694272/74321 694282*

comments

The recent publication of this Austrian Radio tape brings us the first post-war stage performance of the opera in its re-opened birthplace.

It also gives the chance to experience the Barak of the veteran Ludwig Weber, who was replaced for Decca's subsequent studio recording (performance no 5) by the more youthful sounding Paul Schöffler.

Although lacking the ultimate in orchestral detail of that Decca version, the performance nonetheless preserves an important moment in the Staatsoper's distinguished history.

performance no 5

kaiserin	**leonie rysanek**
färberin	**christel goltz**
amme	**elisabeth höngen**
kaiser	**hans hopf**
barak	**paul schöffler**
geisterbote	**kurt böhme**
stimme des falken	**judith hellwig**
erscheinung eines jünglings	**karl terkal**
hüter der schwelle	**emmy loose**
stimme von oben	**hilde rössl-majdan**
der einäugige	**harald pröglhöf**
der einarmige	**oskar czerwenka**
der bucklige	**murray dickie**

performance no 5

date	29 november-10 december 1955
venue	grosser musikvereinssaal wien
orchestra	wiener philharmoniker
choirs	chor der wiener staatsoper
conductor	**karl böhm**
catalogue numbers	lp: decca LXT 5180-5184/GOM 554-557/ GOS 554-557/london (usa) XLLA 46/ A 4505/SRS 64503/telefunken 635.114/ barclay 591.132 cd: decca 425 9812 *excerpts on lp: decca 414 1771/telefunken BLK 16521/london (usa) OS 26205 and cd: decca 440 3602*

comments

Rumour has it that this Decca studio recording, which would remain the only one of its kind for many years to come, was made with great insistence and sacrifice from the conductor and principals, who had just completed a successful run of performances for the opening of the re-built Staatsoper (performance no 4).

It represented a considerable marketing risk for a record company, originally appearing on five mono lps at a time when there were still few complete available versions of the Wagner music dramas, let alone the more esoteric stage works of Richard Strauss.

Ludwig Weber, who sang the role of Barak on stage, was not available to record the part for Decca due to a prior contractual commitment to Columbia's Walter Legge.

performance no 6

kaiserin	**gundula janowitz**
färberin	**gladys kuchta**
amme	**grace hoffman**
kaiser	**jess thomas**
barak	**otto wiener**
geisterbote	**walter kreppel**
stimme des falken	**lucia popp**
erscheinung eines jünglings	**ermanno lorenzi**
hüter der schwelle	**lucia popp**
stimme von oben	**margarita lilowa**
der einäugige	**siegfried rudolf frese**
der einarmige	**ludwig welter**
der bucklige	**erich majkut**

41
performance no 6

date	8 june 1964/dress rehearsal performance
venue	staatsoper wien
orchestra	orchester der wiener staatsoper
choirs	chor der wiener staatsoper
conductor	**herbert von karajan**
catalogue numbers	cd: gala GL 100.607/OOA 4493/ opera depot 10213

comments

Originally thought to be a second performance on 17 june 1964, this is clearly an in-house taping of a dress rehearsal in less vivid sound than the broadcast of the premiere on 11 june (performance no 7).

However, it does give us glimpses of some of the alternative (double) cast – the controversial casting of the young Gundula Janowitz as Kaiserin (obviously a role she would never repeat without the careful nurturing of conductor Herbert von Karajan) and the far more conventional, less youthful, Färberpaar of Gladys Kuchta and Otto Wiener.

Miracles of orchestral sonority can still be heard from time to time through the rather dim acoustic.

performance no 7

kaiserin	**leonie rysanek**
färberin	**christa ludwig**
amme	**grace hoffman**
kaiser	**jess thomas**
barak	**walter berry**
geisterbote	**walter kreppel**
stimme des falken	**lucia popp**
erscheinung eines jünglings	**fritz wunderlich**
hüter der schwelle	**lucia popp**
stimme von oben	**margarita lilowa**
der einäugige	**siegfried rudolf frese**
der einarmige	**ludwig welter**
der bucklige	**erich majkut**

Austrian critic Karl Löbl wrote of the performance :-
"under Karajan's direction the music shone out in all its magnificence and glory, with a rich beauty so perfect and inspired that one had to ask onself at times whether such beauty of sound was actually possible. It was the greatest evening of Karajan's conducting career: like a virtuoso at the keyboard of the finest instrument, he coaxed out subtle, impressionistic details, the broad flow of melody and thrilling climaxes, showing again how completely he understands all the possibilities of this theatre........"

43

performance no 7

date	11 june 1964/public performance
venue	staatsoper wien
orchestra	orchester der wiener staatsoper
choirs	chor der wiener staatsoper
conductor	**herbert von karajan**
catalogue numbers	cd: nuova era NE 2288-2290/arkadia CDKAR 207/deutsche grammophon 457 6782/TOLFRAU 196401

comments

This was Karajan's last new production in his directorship of the Wiener Staatsoper, performed precisely on the hundredth birthday of the composer. it was a remarkable first night, recorded in fulsome mono sound by Austrian Radio and greeted in ecstatic terms by the Viennese critics who were normally readier than most to find fault (see an example on the opposite page).

In the face of the eulogies, I feel that too much is made of the fact that Karajan makes many standard cuts and, in the second act, has the solo scenes for Kaiser and Kaiserin placed together whilst the Barak scenes are merged into one.

Husband and wife team Walter Berry and Christa Ludwig were making their role debuts as a Färberpaar which sounds more youthful than most who had been heard previously in the parts in Vienna or elsewhere. Leonie Rysanek excelled her usual impassioned self in one of her many outings in the part of Kaiserin, Grace Hoffman portrayed the Amme without any trace of caricature, whilst real star quality was in evidence in the casting of Lucia Popp and Fritz Wunderlich in smaller roles.

performance no 8

kaiserin	**leonie rysanek**
färberin	**christa ludwig**
amme	**ruth hesse**
kaiser	**james king**
barak	**walter berry**
geisterbote	**martin egel**
stimme des falken	**maria haug**
erscheinung eines jünglings	**martin schomberg**
hüter der schwelle	**maria haug**
stimme von oben	**ingrid mayr**
der einäugige	**zoltan kelemen**
der einarmige	**lorenzo alvary**
der bucklige	**murray dickie**

performance no 8

date	16 august 1974/public performance
venue	grosses festspielhaus salzburg
orchestra	wiener philharmoniker
choirs	chor der wiener staatsoper
conductor	**karl böhm**
catalogue numbers	cd: opera d'oro OPD 1218/OPD 7026/ house of opera CDBB 573/ premiere opera 279 *excerpts from the recording also on cd gala GL 100.607*

comments

The transfer to disc of what was probably an acceptable radio broadcast sound quality has been carried out in such a way as to make this a very difficult listen: whilst the orchestral contribution retains some presence, the voices possess a somewhat dead quality.

This is a pity as the performance was Salzburg's first presentation of the piece since 1933 and gave Europe a chance to hear conductor Böhm's chosen quartet of Rysanek/Ludwig/King/Berry, which had become his standard casting at the Metropolitan Opera in New York.

performanc no 9

kaiserin	**leonie rysanek**
färberin	**ursula schröder-feinen**
amme	**ruth hesse**
kaiser	**james king**
barak	**walter berry**
geisterbote	**robert kerns**
stimme des falken	**maria haug**
erscheinung eines jünglings	**martin schomberg**
hüter der schwelle	**loretta di franco**
stimme von oben	**ingrid mayr**
der einäugige	**zoltan kelemen**
der einarmige	**lorenzo alvary**
der bucklige	**murray dickie**

47
performance no 9

date 26 july 1975/public performance

venue grosses festspielhaus salzburg

orchestra wiener philharmoniker

choirs chor der wiener staatsoper

conductor **karl böhm**

catalogue numbers cd: link 614/bella voce BLV 107 245
excerpts from acts one and two of the recording also on cd gala GL 100.583

comments

This good quality tape of the Austrian Radio broadcast yielded a major cast change following Christa Ludwig's decision to abandon most of the hochdramatisch roles in her repertoire: the part of Färberin was now taken by Ursula Schröder-Feinen, thrillingly reckless in the character's many outbursts and with a memorable contribution to the work's concluding quartet

performance no 10

kaiserin	**leonie rysanek**
färberin	**birgit nilsson**
amme	**ruth hesse**
kaiser	**james king**
barak	**walter berry**
geisterbote	**peter wimberger**
stimme des falken	**lotte rysanek**
erscheinung eines jünglings	**ewald aichberger**
hüter der schwelle	**lotte rysanek**
stimme von oben	**gertrude jahn**
der einäugige	**hans helm**
der einarmige	**lorenzo alvary**
der bucklige	**murray dickie**

performance no 10

date	23 october 1977/public performance
venue	staatsoper wien
orchestra	orchester der wiener staatsoper
choirs	chor der wiener staatsoper
conductor	**karl böhm**
catalogue numbers	lp: historical recording enterprises HRE 322/ deutsche grammophon 415 4731 cd: deutsche grammophon 415 4732/ 445 3252/445 4912

comments

Under Böhm's guidance, Birgit Nilsson manages to get more under the skin of the Färberin than on her previous effort under Sawallisch (performance no. 23).
This was at a time when she was opera's leading Elektra, a role to whose brilliance she was far better suited than the enigmatic Färberin. Nilsson tells in her memoirs how she was first attracted to the part of Kaiserin but that Böhm persuaded her otherwise: the singer was convinced when she first heard Rysanek's Kaiserin and knew that she could not compete !

Austrian Radio, from whom Deutsche Grammophon "borrowed" the tapes in order to complete the veteran Böhm's recorded Strauss cycle for the label, achieve a fine balance between voices and the Philharmoniker, still billing themselves modestly as Orchester der Wiener Staatsoper.

This revival, which carried on with performances into the summer of 1978, constituted Böhm's final confrontation with the score in the house for which it had been written. Between 1943 and 1978 he conducted all but three of the opera's performances in the Wiener Staatsoper: a more fitting consummation of his devotion to Richard Strauss could not be hoped for.

Deutsche Grammophon describe the recording as having been made at more than one performance, and indeed a second Austrian Radio tape dated 27 October does apparently survive.

performance no 11

kaiserin	**leonie rysanek**
färberin	**gwyneth jones**
amme	**ruth hesse**
kaiser	**james king**
barak	**walter berry**
geisterbote	**robert kerns**
stimme des falken	**lotte rysanek**
erscheinung eines jünglings	**john dickie**
hüter der schwelle	**marjorie vance**
stimme von oben	**gertrude jahn**
der einäugige	**georg tichy**
der einarmige	**rudolf mazzola**
der bucklige	**helmut wildhaber**

performance no 11

date	6 november 1984/public performance
venue	staatsoper wien
orchestra	orchester der wiener staatsoper
choirs	chor der wiener staatsoper
conductor	**christoph von dohnanyi**
catalogue numbers	cd: premiere opera 02369

comments

An in-house recording of very acceptable quality, this seems to have been the work's first revival since the death of Karl Böhm in 1981. A cast which in the main had been used to working with him here adapts well to the new maestro. He is a conducting figure whom I personally find far less inspiring than the older school of Kapellmeister.

Leonie Rysanek still turns in a tour de force in the signature role which she was very soon to relinquish after performing it for an astonishing thirty years, whilst Walter Berry was soon to abandon his hold on the part of Barak which had lasted for a full twenty years.

performance no 12

kaiserin	**julia varady**
färberin	**hildegard behrens**
amme	**reinhild runkel**
kaiser	**placido domingo**
barak	**jose van dam**
geisterbote	**albert dohmen**
stimme des falken	**sumi jo**
erscheinung eines jünglings	**robert gambill**
hüter der schwelle	**eva lind**
stimme von oben	**elzbieta ardam**
der einäugige	**gottfried hornik**
der einarmige	**hans franzen**
der bucklige	**wilfried gahmlich**

performance no 12

date	march, april and september 1989 and october 1991
venue	konzerthaus wien
orchestra	wiener philharmoniker
choirs	konzertvereinigung wiener staatsopernchor and wiener sängerknaben
conductor	**georg solti**
catalogue numbers	cd: decca 436 2432/458 7002

comments

This is the first recording of the piece to have been made without the co-operation of a radio station or in conjunction with concurrent stage performances. The conductor proudly notes in the accompanying booklet that every note written by Strauss has been recorded, a claim which few others were to make.

Also vaunted by Decca to have been their most costly project to date, certainly no expense has been spared in achieving a miraculous sound quality, showcasing orchestral virtuosity of the highest order.

Vocally, however, there is little comparison to be made with Decca's 1955 casting (performance no 5), when all the principals are heard to be fully inside their roles: here Kaiser, Barak and Amme seem to be sightreading their parts. Only Julia Varady as Kaiserin measures up to her illustrious predecessors, giving a most impassioned account of the difficult role: she may not have sung the role on stage, but as with virtually everything she sang for the gramophone she penetrates to the heart of the elusive character, even surpassing the ubiquitous Rysanek in terms of pure vocal beauty.

performance no 13

kaiserin	**cheryl studer**
färberin	**eva marton**
amme	**marjana lipovsek**
kaiser	**thomas moser**
barak	**robert hale**
geisterbote	**bryn terfel**
stimme des falken	**andrea rost**
erscheinung eines jünglings	**herbert lippert**
hüter der schwelle	**elisabeth norberg-schulz**
stimme von oben	**elzbieta ardam**
der einäugige	**manfred hemm**
der einarmige	**hans franzen**
der bucklige	**wilfried gahmlich**

performance no 13

date	july 1992/public performance
venue	grosses festspielhaus salzburg
orchestra	wiener philharmoniker
choirs	konzertvereinigung wiener staatsopernchor and salzburger kinderchor
conductor	**georg solti**
catalogue numbers	lasedisc: decca 071 4251 vhs video: decca 071 4253 dvd video: decca 071 4259

comments

In many ways preferable to Solti's studio recording of three years earlier (performance no 12), this live television performance stands up well when heard without the picture: in fact its musical values are better appreciated without visual distraction. The eventful musical landscape flows effortlessly by in a way that it does not in that studio edition.

The cast I would describe as impeccable, with absolutely no weak links and the bonus of a fresh-voiced Geisterbote from Bryn Terfel in what must have been one of his first international appearances. I must also admit that Eva Marton portrays the Färberin with far more appeal than in her various other performances of the part.

performance no 14

kaiserin	**deborah voigt**
färberin	**gabriele schnaut**
amme	**marjana lipovsek**
kaiser	**johan botha**
barak	**falk struckmann**
geisterbote	**wolfgang bankl**
stimme des falken	**rachel harnisch**
erscheinung eines jünglings	**johan botha**
hüter der schwelle	**rachel harnisch**
stimme von oben	**regina mauel**
der einäugige	**geert smits**
der einarmige	**peter köves**
der bucklige	**herwig pecoraro**

performance no 14

date	11 december 1999/public performance
venue	staatsoper wien
orchestra	orchester der wiener staatsoper
choirs	chor der wiener staatsoper
conductor	**giuseppe sinopoli**
catalogue numbers	cd: private edition vienna/premiere opera 031363

comments

Vividly recorded by Austrian Radio, conductor Sinopoli goes on to improve on his first efforts in 1996 (Turin and Dresden). Perfect balances reveal a refulgent Wiener Philharmoniker and a fine singing team, in which Falk Struckmann stands out as one of the finest Baraks, combining Fischer-Dieskau's nobility with Berry's open earthiness.

performance no 15

kaiserin	**deborah voigt**
färberin	**gabriele schnaut**
amme	**jane henschel**
kaiser	**ben heppner**
barak	**falk struckmann**
geisterbote	**wolfgang bankl**
stimme des falken	**rachel harnisch**
erscheinung eines jünglings	**ben heppner**
hüter der schwelle	**rachel harnisch**
stimme von oben	**regina mauel**
der einäugige	**geert smits**
der einarmige	**peter köves**
der bucklige	**herwig pecoraro**

performance no 15

date	6 may 2000/public performance
venue	staatsoper wien
orchestra	orchester der wiener staatsoper
choirs	chor der wiener staatsoper
conductor	**giuseppe sinopoli**
catalogue numbers	cd: handelman 09253

comments

Dimly recorded in-house tape of a second performance in the same season (performance no 14), with two major cast changes in Jane Henschel and Ben Heppner. Fortunately, both can be heard to better advantage in recordings elsewhere.

performance no 16

kaiserin	**anne schwanewilms**
färberin	**evelyn herlitzius**
amme	**michaela schuster**
kaiser	**stephen gould**
barak	**wolfgang koch**
geisterbote	**thomas johannes mayer**
stimme des falken	**rachel frenkel**
erscheinung eines jünglings	**peter sonn**
hüter der schwelle	**christiana landshamer**
stimme von oben	**maria radner**
der einäugige	**markus brück**
der einarmige	**steven humes**
der bucklige	**andreas conrad**

performance no 16

date	29 july 2011/public performance
venue	grosses festspielhaus salzburg
orchestra	wiener philharmoniker
choirs	konzertvereinigung wiener staatsopernchor and salzburger kinderchor
conductor	**christian thielemann**
catalogue numbers	cd: private edition vienna *dvd awaiting publication*

comments

Not since the performances of this very opera at the Wiener Staatsoper in June 1964 (performance nos 6 and 7) have the Wiener Philharmoniker achieved such a fusion of visceral power and absolute perfection (one thinks of the description "controlled ecstasy" coined by the writer Peter Csobadi when discussing Herbert von Karajan). All of Christian Thielemann's performances of the Richard Strauss score up to this date (see Berlin and New York) can be heard as a preparation for what takes place in Salzburg in July 2011.

The cast is in perfect unison with its conductor, particularly on the female side. Evelyn Herlitzius manages power and feminity in equal measure, Michaela Schuster is malevolent without sounding superannuated, whilst Anne Schwanewilms, her less than large soprano supported by a conductor who really understands singers, achieves what only Gundula Janowitz did for Karajan in 1964 – combining brilliance with youthful vulnerability, and her handling of the crucial spoken dialogue in Act 3 when the Kaiserin ultimately refuses to drink the water of life, must be heard to be believed.

performance no 17

kaiserin	**deborah voigt**
färberin	**sabine hass**
amme	**hanna schwarz**
kaiser	**ben heppner**
barak	**franz grundheber**
geisterbote	**hans-joachim ketelsen**
stimme des falken	**sabine brohm**
erscheinung eines jünglings	**werner güra**
hüter der schwelle	**ute selbig**
stimme von oben	**nadja michael**
der einäugige	**andreas scheibner**
der einarmige	**andre eckert**
der bucklige	**roland wagenführer**

performance no 17

date	november-december 1996/public performances
venue	semperoper dresden
orchestra	sächsische staatskapelle dresden
choirs	chor der sächsischen staatsoper
conductor	**giuseppe sinopoli**
catalogue numbers	cd: warner classics 0630 131562

comments

Dresden conductors associated with the work in its early performing history included Fritz Reiner (Dresden premiere), the composer himself (four performances between 1927 and 1934), Karl Böhm and Karl Elmendorff.

After the Second World War, Dresden had to wait sixty years before Die Frau ohne Schatten returned to the stage of the Semperoper. On the evidence of this recording, the wait was worthwhile, with orchestral playing and singing, by modern standards at least, of a high calibre.

Now led by Giuseppe Sinopoli, a self-confessed specialist in the music of decadence, the cast was a distinguished one, although the indisposition of Canadian tenor Ben Heppner meant that some performances of the Kaiser (including two which I attended) were taken by the less alluring voice of Heinz Kruse.

performance no 18

kaiserin	**amanda halgrimson**
färberin	**luana devol**
amme	**hanna schwarz**
kaiser	**reiner goldberg**
barak	**franz grundheber**
geisterbote	**hans joachim ketelsen**
stimme des falken	**sabine brohm**
erscheinung eines jünglings	**gerald hupach**
hüter der schwelle	**christiane hossfeld**
stimme von oben	**christa mayer**
der einäugige	**matthias henneberg**
der einarmige	**andre eckert**
der bucklige	**klaus florian vogt**

performance no 18

date	5 september 2001/public performance
venue	semperoper dresden
orchestra	sächsische staatskapelle dresden
choirs	chor und kinderchor der sächsischen staatsoper
conductor	**marc albrecht**

comments

A rather cavernous in-house recording precludes detailed listening to this performance.

Two veterans of German opera have now joined the cast: former Heldentenor Reiner Goldberg as Kaiser and Hanna Schwarz an authoritative Amme.

performance no 19

kaiserin	**susan anthony**
färberin	**gabriele schnaut**
amme	**ildiko szönyi**
kaiser	**stephen gould**
barak	**jukka rasilainen**
geisterbote	**hans joachim ketelsen**
stimme des falken	**sabine brohm**
erscheinung eines jünglings	**gerald hupach**
hüter der schwelle	**ute selbig**
stimme von oben	**christa mayer**
der einäugige	**matthias henneberg**
der einarmige	**jacques greg belobo**
der bucklige	**tom martinsen**

performance no 19

date	18 september 2004/public performance
venue	semperoper dresden
orchestra	sächsische staatskapelle dresden
choirs	chor und kinderchor der sächsischen staatsoper
conductor	**michael boder**
comments	

This in-house recording introduces us to the striking Salome voice of Susan Anthony and an early appearance as Kaiser of Heldentenor Stephen Gould.

performance no 20

kaiserin	**catherine foster**
färberin	**evelyn herlitzius**
amme	**doris soffel**
kaiser	**stephen gould**
barak	**franz grundheber**
geisterbote	**hans joachim ketelsen**
stimme des falken	**sabine brohm**
erscheinung eines jünglings	**gerald hupach**
hüter der schwelle	**christiane hossfeld**
stimme von oben	**christa mayer**
der einäugige	**matthias henneberg**
der einarmige	**jacques greg belobo**
der bucklige	**tom martinsen**

69
performance no 20

date 26 march 2008/public performance

venue semperoper dresden

orchestra sächsische staatskapelle dresden

choirs chor und kinderchor der sächsischen staatsoper

conductor **michael boder**

comments

A good quality in-house recording, with the inimitable sound of the Staatskapelle and a very strong cast of principals, in particular Doris Soffel, Evelyn Herlitzius and Stephen Gould.

performance no 21

kaiserin	**leonie rysanek**
färberin	**marianne schech**
amme	**lilian benningsen**
kaiser	**hans hopf**
barak	**josef metternich**
geisterbote	**kurt böhme**
stimme des falken	**gerda sommerschuh**
erscheinung eines jünglings	**howard vandenburg**
hüter der schwelle	**erika köth**
stimme von oben	**ina gerhein**
der einäugige	**karl hoppe**
der einarmige	**rudolf wünzer**
der bucklige	**karl ostertag**

performance no 21

date	31 august 1954/public performance
venue	prinzregententheater münchen
orchestra	bayerisches staatsorchester
choirs	chor der bayerischen staatsoper
conductor	**rudolf kempe**
catalogue numbers	lp: melodram MEL 108 cd: voci della luna VL 2007/golden melodram GM 10033/walhall WLCD 0088/premiere opera 497/ TOLFRAU 19540

comments

Having last presented the opera in 1939 with Strauss specialist Clemens Krauss, the 1954 Munich Opera Festival performances were apparently its first post-war staging.

Several cast members would be taking their parts to the re-opening of Vienna's Staatsoper some fifteen months later (performance no. 4), but this is the only opportunity we have to hear Josef Metternich's moving portrayal of Barak.

Rudolf Kempe leads the performance with his famous ability to keep transparent even the densest orchestral textures, thus assuring the singers of a comfortable ride.

A Melodram LP (MEL 085) devoted to Leonie Rysanek contained an extract from a 1956 Munich performance conducted by Meinhard von Zallinger.

performance no 22

kaiserin	**ingrid bjoner**
färberin	**inge borkh**
amme	**martha mödl**
kaiser	**jess thomas**
barak	**dietrich fischer-dieskau**
geisterbote	**hans hotter**
stimme des falken	**gerda sommerschuh**
erscheinung eines jünglings	**georg paskuda**
hüter der schwelle	**ingeborg hallstein**
stimme von oben	**hertha töpper**
der einäugige	**karl hoppe**
der einarmige	**max proebstl**
der bucklige	**paul kuen**

73

performance no 22

date	21 november 1963/performance for invited guests
venue	nationaltheater münchen
orchestra	bayerisches staatsorchester
choirs	chor der bayerischen staatsoper
conductor	**joseph keilberth**
catalogue numbers	lp: deutsche grammophon LPM 18 911-18 914/SLPM 138 911-138 914/2721 161 cd: deutsche grammophon 449 5842 *excerpts from the recording on deutsche grammophon lp SLPEM 136 422*

comments

This live recording was made by Deutsche Grammophon engineers in the rebuilt Nationaltheater two days before the official public opening with Wagner's Meistersinger. Several sequences from the performance were also recorded for television (presumably at rehearsal) and one of them can be seen in a DVD devoted to Dietrich Fischer-Dieskau (Deutsche Grammophon 073 4050).

This is a cast with very few weak links: in addition to Fischer-Dieskau's Barak, an impressive Kaiserin from Bjoner, a thrilling Mödl as Amme and no less a figure than Hotter as Geisterbote – although conductor Keilberth tells us in his memoirs (Ein Dirigentenleben im 20. Jahrhundert) that Hotter's contributions had to be re-recorded and dubbed into the final tape due to the singer's very bad cold on the day of the performance.

Like Kempe before him, Keilberth achieves marvellous sonorities whilst keeping the heaviest scoring always singer-friendly.

performance no 23

kaiserin	**ingrid bjoner**
färberin	**birgit nilsson**
amme	**astrid varnay**
kaiser	**james king**
barak	**dietrich fischer-dieskau**
geisterbote	**karl christian kohn**
stimme des falken	**antonia fahberg**
erscheinung eines jünglings	**norbert orth**
hüter der schwelle	**ruth falcon**
stimme von oben	**gudrun wewezow**
der einäugige	**hermann sapell**
der einarmige	**karl helm**
der bucklige	**lorenz fehenberger**

performance no 23

date	29 september 1976/public performance
venue	nationaltheater münchen
orchestra	bayerisches staatsorchester
choirs	chor der bayerischen staatsoper
conductor	**wolfgang sawallisch**
catalogue numbers	lp: legendary recordings LR 202 cd: legendary recordings LRCD 1029/ golden melodram GM 30033/house of opera CDBB 570/opera-lover FRAU 197 601/*some issues dated 3 october 1976*

comments

Frau became very much a repertory piece for the Bayerisches Staatsoper, and here it is attentively played and sung by a well versed team of singers, with the inimitable Varnay very much a commanding presence at its centre.

For me personally the Färberin of Birgit Nilsson is a stumbling block: whilst she captures the character's shrewishness well enough, there is no sign of the warmth and vulnerability which was brought out so well by singers like Christel Goltz or Christa Ludwig.

performance no 24

kaiserin	**mechthild gessendorf**
färberin	**ingrid bjoner**
amme	**helga dernesch**
kaiser	**robert schunk**
barak	**theo adam**
geisterbote	**roland bracht**
stimme des falken	**antonia fahberg**
erscheinung eines jünglings	**norbert orth**
hüter der schwelle	**cheryl studer**
stimme von oben	**gudrun wewezow**
der einäugige	**hermann sapell**
der einarmige	**karl helm**
der bucklige	**georg paskuda**

performance no 24

date 28 december 1981/public performance

venue nationaltheater münchen

orchestra bayerisches staatsorchester

choirs chor der bayerischen staatsoper

conductor **wolfgang sawallisch**

comments

This very acceptable in-house recording brings us the noble Barak of Theo Adam, Ingrid Bjoner now as Färberin and a new Kaiserpaar in Mechthild Gessendorf and Robert Schunk – the latter a very cool Kaiser who sounds from the start as if he were already turned to stone !

Masterly conducting from Sawallisch, who served the opera over a long period in Munich just as Böhm had done in Vienna and New York

performance no 25

kaiserin	**sabine hass**
färberin	**ingrid bjoner**
amme	**ute trekel-burkhardt**
kaiser	**james king**
barak	**theo adam**
geisterbote	**jan hendrik rootering**
stimme des falken	**marianne seibel**
erscheinung eines jünglings	**claes ahnsjö**
der einäugige	**hermann sapell**
der einarmige	**karl helm**
der bucklige	**georg paskuda**

performance no 25

date	21 november 1984/public performance
venue	nationaltheater münchen
orchestra	bayerisches staatsorchester
choirs	chor der bayerischen staatsoper
conductor	**wolfgang sawallisch**
catalogue numbers	cd: house of opera CDBB 571/ audio encyclopedia AE 004

comments

In-house recording of average quality, but again revealing filigree playing from Wolfgang Sawallisch and his orchestral forces.

Two of the principals represent the high quality of singing to be heard in the German Democratic Republic at that time: Theo Adam's Barak is now joined by an impressive Amme from Ute Trekel-Burkhardt

performance no 26

kaiserin	**cheryl studer**
färberin	**ute vinzing**
amme	**hanna schwarz**
kaiser	**rene kollo**
barak	**alfred muff**
geisterbote	**andreas schmidt**
stimme des falken	**julie kaufmann**
erscheinung eines jünglings	**paul frey**
hüter der schwelle	**cyndia sieden**
stimme von oben	**marjana lipovsek**
der einäugige	**jan hendrik rootering**
der einarmige	**kurt rydl**
der bucklige	**kenneth garrison**

81
performance no 26

date	february, march, october and november 1987
venue	herkulessaal der münchner residenz
orchestra	sinfonie-orchester des bayerischen rundfunks
choirs	chor des bayerischen rundfunks and tölzer knabenchor
conductor	**wolfgang sawallisch**
catalogue numbers	lp: emi 749 0741 cd: emi 749 0742/754 4942

comments

Billed as the first ever complete gramophone recording, EMI had presumably got wind of Decca's plans for a version with Georg Solti, and with this co-production with Bayerischer Rundfunk stole the rival company's thunder by getting onto the market before them.

Although most of the cast had stage experience of their roles, the result remains a trifle studied and fails to rival some of the live performances from the Bayerische Staatsoper or elsewhere.

For a really inspired reading of the uncut score on record, one must go back to 1950 (Winfried Zillig in Frankfurt-am-Main) or forward to Christian Thielemann (1999-2011).

performance no 27

kaiserin	**cheryl studer**
färberin	**gwyneth jones**
amme	**brigitte fassbänder**
kaiser	**robert schunk**
barak	**bernd weikl**
geisterbote	**jan hendrik rootering**
stimme des falken	**julia faulkner**
erscheinung eines jünglings	**claes ahnsjö**
hüter der schwelle	**angela maria blasi**
stimme von oben	**birgit calm**
der einäugige	**hermann sapell**
der einarmige	**kieth engen**
der bucklige	**georg paskuda**

performance no 27

date	12 july 1988/public performance
venue	nationaltheater münchen
orchestra	bayerisches staatsorchester
choirs	chor der bayerischen staatsoper
conductor	**wolfgang sawallisch**
comments	

Good quality in-house recording, in which Cheryl Studer far excels her studio effort as Kaiserin, Brigitte Fassbänder contributes fresh insights into the part of Amme and Gwyneth Jones is a riveting and fairly firm-voiced Färberin.

The performance is conducted by Sawallisch with a power not found in that studio version (performance no 26), although the score of Act 3 is here still quite heavily cut.

performance no 28

kaiserin	**cheryl studer**
färberin	**ingrid bjoner**
amme	**helga dernesch**
kaiser	**robert schunk**
barak	**alfred muff**
geisterbote	**jan hendrik rootering**
stimme des falken	**julia faulkner**
erscheinung eines jünglings	**claes ahnsjö**
hüter der schwelle	**angela maria blasi**
stimme von oben	**birgit calm**
der einäugige	**hermann sapell**
der einarmige	**karl helm**
der bucklige	**georg paskuda**

performance no 28

date	16 july 1988/public performance
venue	nationaltheater münchen
orchestra	bayerisches staatsorchester
choirs	chor der bayerischen staatsoper
conductor	**wolfgang sawallisch**
catalogue numbers	cd: house of opera CDBB 574/ audio encyclopedia AE 004

comments

Such was the affluence of the Bavarians that during their showcase Opernfestspiele they were able to muster three cast changes in major roles in a performance only four days after performance no 27.

Sadly none of these changes are for the better: Helga Dernesch is an uneasy Amme, Alfred Muff a gruff-sounding Barak and Ingrid Bjoner now sadly in vocal decline as Färberin (reflecting the fate of her fellow Scandinavian Birgit Nilsson in that very same part).

performance no 29

kaiserin	**luana devol**
färberin	**janis martin**
amme	**marjana lipovsek**
kaiser	**peter seiffert**
barak	**alan titus**
geisterbote	**jan hendrik rootering**
stimme des falken	**caroline maria petrig**
erscheinung eines jünglings	**herbert lippert**
hüter der schwelle	**annegeer stumphius**
stimme von oben	**anne salvan**
der einäugige	**hermann sapell**
der einarmige	**alfred kuhn**
der bucklige	**kevin conners**

performance no 29

date	8 and 11 november 1992/public performances
venue	aichi prefecture art theatre nagoya
orchestra	bayerisches staatsorchester
choirs	chor der bayerischen staatsoper
conductor	**wolfgang sawallisch**
catalogue numbers	dvd: tdk DVWW-OPFROS/ arthaus 107 245

comments

The work obviously held a special place in the Richard Strauss canon for conductor Sawallisch, who conducted it throughout his tenure at the Bayerische Staatsoper. It was therefore fitting that his final performances of this opera before relinquishing his post should be a new production, mounted jointly with Japanese forces and premiered during the Staatsoper's visit to Japan in 1992.

This DVD stems from a planned TV recording, which in the event was not transmitted due to the intervention of the Japanese censor, who had moral objections to the opera's subject matter. Beautiful sets give a suitably oriental flavour, whilst the soundtrack reveals a homogeneous and well-drilled ensemble with no weak links.

Outstanding is the American soprano Luana Devol, who with this performance as Kaiserin as well as later ones as Färberin assumes an important place in the work's recorded history.

Munich performances of this production after the retirement of Sawallisch were in the hands of Christof Prick and Peter Schneider (performance no 30).

performance no 30

kaiserin	**inga nielsen**
färberin	**deborah polaski**
amme	**marjana lipovsek**
kaiser	**alan woodrow**
barak	**wolfgang brendel**
geisterbote	**harry dworchak**
stimme des falken	**caroline maria petrig**
erscheinung eines jünglings	**claes ahnsjö**
hüter der schwelle	**annegeer stumphius**
stimme von oben	**silvia fichtl**
der einäugige	**jan zinkler**
der einarmige	**alfred kuhn**
der bucklige	**kevin connors**

performance no 30

date	30 september 2000/public performance
venue	nationaltheater münchen
orchestra	bayerisches staatsorchester
choirs	chor der bayerischen staatsoper
conductor	**peter schneider**
comments	

In this high quality in-house recording, a reliable cast ensures that everything is in place for a smooth – perhaps a little uneventful – passage through Strauss's score under the aegis of Kapellmeister Schneider.

performance no 31

kaiserin	**hildegard hillebrecht**
färberin	**gladys kuchta**
amme	**ruth hesse**
kaiser	**james king**
barak	**gerd feldhoff**
geisterbote	**hubert hoffmann**
stimme des falken	**catherine gayer**
erscheinung eines jünglings	**loren driscoll**
hüter der schwelle	**marina turke**
stimme von oben	**sieglinde wagner**
der einäugige	**ernst krukowski**
der einarmige	**manfred röhrl**
der bucklige	**martin vantin**

performance no 31

date	9 june 1964/public performance
venue	deutsche oper berlin
orchestra	orchester der deutschen oper
choirs	chor der deutschen oper
conductor	**karl böhm**

comments

Premiered the previous February under Böhm, this Berlin production was part of the Richard Strauss centenary celebrations.

James King takes the role of Kaiser, with which he was to become closely associated over the next twenty years. Hildegard Hillebrecht reveals as Kaiserin a more flexible and youthful sounding voice than in her later performances at Covent Garden. Gerd Feldhoff is a noble and deeply felt Barak, his wife being taken by the underrated dramatic soprano of American origin, Gladys Kuchta – she was highly valued in the 1960s in the German repertoire.

Taut and vividly projected conducting from Karl Böhm, no less successful than his many Vienna and North American readings.

performance no 32

kaiserin	**enriquetta tarres**
färberin	**ludmila dvorakova**
amme	**sigrid kehl**
kaiser	**martin ritzmann**
barak	**antonin svorc**
geisterbote	**siegfried vogel**
stimme des falken	**jutta vulpius**
erscheinung eines jünglings	**harald neukirch**
hüter der schwelle	**jutta vulpius**
stimme von oben	**gertraud prenzlow**
der einäugige	**erich siebenschuh**
der einarmige	**günther fröhlich**
der bucklige	**joachim arndt**

performance no 32

date	21 March 1971/public performance
venue	deutsche staatsoper berlin-ost
orchestra	staatskapelle berlin
choirs	chor der deutschen staatsoper
conductor	**otmar suitner**

comments

Although the surviving recording is rough and with certain passages missing from the radio transmission, it is worth persevering to experience an old-fashioned declamatory style of singing this music – in other words, the best of DDR music-making.

Another performance from East Berlin (1984) is listed in the section devoted to performances not actually auditioned.

performance no 33

kaiserin	**leonie rysanek**
färberin	**ute vinzing**
amme	**ruth hesse**
kaiser	**gerd brenneis**
barak	**gerd feldhoff**
geisterbote	**william dooley**
stimme des falken	**catherine gayer**
erscheinung eines jünglings	**loren driscoll**
hüter der schwelle	**dorothea weiss**
stimme von oben	**vera little**
der einäugige	**manfred röhrl**
der einarmige	**ernst krukowski**
der bucklige	**martin vantin**

performance no 33

date 25 february 1981/public performance

venue deutsche oper berlin

orchestra orchester der deutschen oper

choirs chor der deutschen oper

conductor **heinrich hollreiser**

comments

The restricted acoustic of this in-house recording does not disguise the fact that here is a performance of some considerable stature.

Conductor Hollreiser delivers a broad symphonic reading of the score, and Leonie Rysanek is still mightily impressive in her signature role, partnered with a noble Färberin in Ute Vinzing.

performance no 34

kaiserin	**sabine hass**
färberin	**janis martin**
amme	**ruth hesse**
kaiser	**gerd brenneis**
barak	**gerd feldhoff**
geisterbote	**william dooley**
stimme des falken	**catherine gayer**
erscheinung eines jünglings	**william pell**
hüter der schwelle	**lucy peacock**
stimme von oben	**kaja borris**
der einäugige	**peter gougaloff**
der einarmige	**william murray**
der bucklige	**manfred röhrl**

performance no 34

date	11 may 1986/public performance
venue	deutsche oper berlin
orchestra	orchester der deutschen oper
choirs	chor der deutschen oper
conductor	**heinrich hollreiser**
comments	

Recorded in-house but of acceptable quality, this is repertory opera of the highest quality.

Kaiserin and Färberin stand out among an even cast of principals. Even the less melifluous voices — Gerd Brenneis and Ruth Hesse — are integrated into a sensitive account of the score, led by an experienced man of the theatre, Heinrich Hollreiser.

performance no 35

kaiserin	**alessandra marc**
färberin	**luana devol**
amme	**jane henschel**
kaiser	**thomas moser**
barak	**wolfgang brendel**
geisterbote	**lenus carlson**
stimme des falken	**fionnula maccarthy**
erscheinung eines jünglings	**marc clear**
hüter der schwelle	**lucy peacock**
stimme von oben	**ulrike hetzel**
der einäugige	**ralf lukas**
der einarmige	**manfred röhrl**
der bucklige	**uwe peper**

performance no 35

date	20 november 1999/public performance
venue	deutsche oper berlin
orchestra	orchester der deutschen oper
choirs	chor der deutschen oper
conductor	**christian thielemann**

comments

One of the musical highlights of Christian Thielemann's tenure at the Deutsche Oper, alongside his traversal of the mature Wagner music dramas, must be the eighteen performances of Frau ohne Schatten which he conducted between 26 September 1998 and 26 January 2005. I was lucky enough to attend a total of eight of these.

Despite frequent changes in principal singers over the seven-year run (one constant was the Amme of Jane Henschel), a close acoustic in the mostly in-house recordings does not disguise that these were truly memorable performances. Both diction and projection recalls a byegone age, and just to single out the second orchestral transition in the first act, this becomes a veritable Hexenritt in Thielemann's hands.

Alessandra Marc's Act Three scene as Kaiserin (Vater bist du's?) must also be singled out as mightily impressive.

performance no 36

kaiserin	**sylvie valayre**
färberin	**gabriele schnaut**
amme	**jane henschel**
kaiser	**thomas moser**
barak	**wolfgang schöne**
geisterbote	**lenus carlson**
stimme des falken	**fionnula maccarthy**
erscheinung eines jünglings	**yosep kang**
hüter der schwelle	**lucy peacock**
stimme von oben	**kari hamnoy**
der einäugige	**yu chen**
der einarmige	**roland schubert**
der bucklige	**burkhard ulrich**

performance no 36

date 28 december 2003/public performance

venue deutsche oper berlin

orchestra orchester der deutschen oper

choirs chor der deutschen oper

conductor **christian thielemann**

comments

This later performance from Christian Thielemann's Berlin series, although in less good recorded quality, nonetheless illustrates how his forces have progressed to even greater heights of orchestral mastery in the five years since they first played the score together.

performance no 37

kaiserin	**annelies kupper**
färberin	**erna schlüter**
amme	**diana eustrati**
kaiser	**heinrich bensing**
barak	**karl kronenberg**
geisterbote	**günther ambrosius**
stimme des falken	**christa ludwig**
erscheinung eines jünglings	**joachim stein**
hüter der schwelle	**maria madler-madsen**
stimme von oben	**käthe lindloff**
der einäugige	**rolf heide**
der einarmige	**sanders schier**
der bucklige	**joachim stein**

.

performance no 37

date	1950/concert performance for radio
venue	sendesaal des hessischen rundfunks frankfurt-am-main
orchestra	sinfonieorchester des hessischen rundfunks
choirs	chor des hessischen rundfunks
conductor	**winfried zillig**
catalogue numbers	cd: ponto PO 1015 *also published on cd by cantus classics*

comments

This excellently recorded radio transmission, free of the restraints of stage movement, enshrines what must be one of the very first complete renditions of the score. It raises the question whether the composer himself, who had died only a year prior to this performance, ever heard it played without the cuts which he had sanctioned.

Inspired performances from all five principals, notwithstanding a dry start from Kronenberg. There is firm dramatic thrust from Schlüter, and a radiant Kaiserin from Kupper. The twenty-one year old Christa Ludwig, later a notable Färberin (not, as Ponto's booklet claims, a Kaiserin), can be heard here as Stimme des Falken.

On this showing the internationally unknown Winfried Zillig well supports the claim to be a Kapellmeister of the very highest order.

performance no 38

kaiserin	**trude eipperle**
färberin	**maria kinas**
amme	**res fischer**
kaiser	**wolfgang windgassen**
barak	**wilhelm schirp**
geisterbote	**gustav neidlinger**

remainder of cast could not be established

performance no 38

date	11 september 1954/public performance
venue	württembergisches staatstheater stuttgart
orchestra	württembergisches staatsorchester
choirs	chor der württembergischen staatsoper
conductor	**ferdinand leitner**
comments	

Primitively recorded and with the orchestra very much in the background, this edition is worth sampling for the Kaiser of Wagnerian supremo Wolfgang Windgassen and the rich contralto of Res Fischer's Amme.

performance no 39

kaiserin	**annemarie leber**
färberin	**liane synek**
amme	**martha mödl**
kaiser	**karl liebl**
barak	**herbert grabe**
geisterbote	**camillo meghor**
stimme des falken	**elisabeth szemzo**
erscheinung eines jünglings	**viktor remsey**
hüter der schwelle	**helga dernesch**
stimme von oben	**elisabeth epperlein**
der einäugige	**heinz peters**
der einarmige	**karl ascher**
der bucklige	**reinhold bartel**

performance no 39

date	1 may 1964/public performance
venue	hessisches landestheater wiesbaden
orchestra	orchester des hessischen landestheaters
choirs	chor des hessischen landestheaters
conductor	**heinz wallberg**

comments

The mediocre quality of this in-house recording makes it very difficult to assess.

However, the larger than life Amme of Martha Mödl does come across, and it is worth sampling both the opening scene as well as the act three sequence for Amme and Kaiserin.

performance no 40

kaiserin	**eva marton**
färberin	**birgit nilsson**
amme	**ruth hesse**
kaiser	**rene kollo**
barak	**donald mcintyre**
geisterbote	**harald stamm**
stimme des falken	**elke andiel**
erscheinung eines jünglings	**heinz kruse**
hüter der schwelle	**yoko kawahara**
stimme von oben	**alicia nafe**
der einäugige	**ude krekow**
der einarmige	**carl schultz**
der bucklige	**peter haage**

performance no 40

date	2 october 1977/public performance
venue	staatsoper hamburg
orchestra	philharmonisches staatsorchester
choirs	chor der staatsoper hamburg
conductor	**christoph von dohnanyi**
catalogue numbers	cd: premiere opera 02312

comments

Moderate in-house recording of what might be described as a "standard" Frau cast of 1970s or 1980s.

Within weeks both Birgit Nilsson and Ruth Hesse would be reprising their roles for Karl Böhm in Vienna (performance no. 10).

I must admit to finding Christoph von Dohnanyi one of the least inspiring of the international conductors who have repeatedly applied themselves to the Frau score.

performance no 41

kaiserin	**eva marton**
färberin	**birgit nilsson**
amme	**ruth hesse**
kaiser	**james king**
barak	**thomas stewart**
geisterbote	**franz grundheber**
stimme des falken	**anne botcher**
erscheinung eines jünglings	**gregory kunde**
hüter der schwelle	**yoko kawahara**
stimme von oben	**alicia nafe**
der einäugige	**ude krekow**
der einarmige	**carl schultz**
der bucklige	**peter haage**

performance no 41

date	8 january 1980/public performance
venue	staatsoper hamburg
orchestra	philharmonisches staatsorchester
choirs	chor der staatsoper hamburg
conductor	**christoph von dohnanyi**

comments

As was the case three years earlier (performance no 40), Dohnanyi guides his reliable international cast through the score with caution rather than passion.

New to the role of Barak is the American bass-baritone Thomas Stewart.

performance no 42

kaiserin	**siw wennberg**
färberin	**gwyneth jones**
amme	**helga dernesch**
kaiser	**robert ilosfalvy**
barak	**walter berry**
geisterbote	**hans günter nöcker**
stimme des falken	**stella kleindienst**
erscheinung eines jünglings	**jean van ree**
hüter der schwelle	**margaret neville**
stimme von oben	**marita knobel**
der einäugige	**klaus bruch**
der einarmige	**ulrich hielscher**
der bucklige	**jean van ree**

113

performance no 42

date	16 march 1980/public performance
venue	oper köln
orchestra	gürzenich-orchester köln
choirs	chor der oper köln
conductor	**john pritchard**
comments	

With Walter Berry as a Barak of some considerable experience, the other main singers are new to their roles in this modest quality in-house recording. All are well guided by orchestra and conductor.

Incidentally, John Pritchard seems to be the first British conductor to have been entrusted with this most Germanic of operas.

performance no 43

kaiserin	**leonie rysanek**
färberin	**gwyneth jones**
amme	**helga dernesch**
kaiser	**robert schunk**
barak	**franz ferdinand nentwig**
geisterbote	**franz grundheber**
stimme des falken	**marianne hirsch**
erscheinung eines jünglings	**heinz kruse**
hüter der schwelle	**yoko kawahara**
stimme von oben	**olive fredericks**
der einäugige	**ude krekow**
der einarmige	**carl schultz**
der bucklige	**frieder stricker**

performance no 43

date	26 december 1983/public performance
venue	staatsoper hamburg
orchestra	philharmonisches staatsorchester
choirs	chor der staatsoper hamburg
conductor	**christoph von dohnanyi**

comments

The rather distant sound on this in-house recording mitigates against the performance making its full impact.

However, it can be clearly heard that Leonie Rysanek and Gwyneth Jones between them dominate the other less forceful principals.

performance no 44

kaiserin	**monica pick-hieronimi**
färberin	**brenda roberts**
amme	**krystina michalowska**
kaiser	**jean cox**
barak	**anthony rafell**
geisterbote	**franz mazura**
stimme des falken	**marussa xyni**
erscheinung eines jünglings	**ion tudoroiu**
hüter der schwelle	**marussa xyni**
stimme von oben	**liljana nejceva**
der einäugige	**gerhard kiepert**
der einarmige	**oskar pürgstaller**
der bucklige	**karlheinz herr**

performance no 44

date	1 may 1987/public performance
venue	nationaltheater mannheim
orchestra	orchester des nationaltheaters mannheim
choirs	chor des nationaltheaters mannheim
conductor	**erich wächter**
comments	

In-house recording of moderate quality but with a strong bias towards the orchestra, it enshrines strong performances from at least three of the principals: Wagner tenor Jean Cox as Kaiser in one of the last appearances of his career, Anthony Rafell as Barak and Brenda Roberts as Färberin.

Standard cuts are made to the score, although at this time they were already being opened up elsewhere in performances or recordings by Erich Leinsdorf, Georg Solti and Wolfgang Sawallisch.

performance no 45

kaiserin	**marilyn howell**
färberin	**janet hardy**
amme	**donna morein**
kaiser	**ronald carter**
barak	**michael dean**
geisterbote	**weldon thomas**
stimme des falken	**elizabeth richards**
erscheinung eines jünglings	**udo scheuerpflug**
hüter der schwelle	**elizabeth richards**
der einäugige	**jochen schmeckenbecher**
der einarmige	**wilhelm prilassnig**
der bucklige	**peter umstadt**

performance no 45

date	2 january 1994/public performance
venue	theater augsburg
orchestra	philharmonisches orchester augsburg
choirs	chor der oper augsburg
conductor	**michael luig**

comments

A performance which illustrates how much many of the provincial German houses had come to rely on singers recruited from the Anglo-Saxon world, with virtually all the principals being English speakers.

Michael Luig conducts this moderate in-house recording in the final year of his directorship of the Augsburg Opera.

The cast is not remarkable, but the voice of Janet Hardy does stand out: the American-born soprano had studied with former Färberin Gladys Kuchta, and performed an impressive Elektra sung for Welsh National Opera during the 1990s.

One does get caught up in this live performance due to the prominently recorded orchestra and some very passionately turned woodwind playing.

performance no 46

kaiserin	**susan anthony**
färberin	**luana devol**
amme	**jane henschel**
kaiser	**jeffrey dowd**
barak	**wolfgang schöne**
geisterbote	**marcel rosca**
stimme des falken	**galina simkina**
erscheinung eines jünglings	**rainer maria rohr**
hüter der schwelle	**galina simkina**
stimme von oben	**gritt gnauck**
der einäugige	**heiko trinsinger**
der einarmige	**almas svilpa**
der bucklige	**herbert hechenberger**

121

performance no 46

date	9 december 2001/public performance
venue	aalto-musiktheater essen
orchestra	essener philharmoniker
choirs	chor des aalto-musiktheaters
conductor	**stefan soltesz**
catalogue numbers	cd: legato classics 534 *legato classics dates the recording as 17 january 2001, which is presumably incorrect*

comments

Ably conducted and recorded in-house, this performance would not be out of place in major houses like Vienna or Berlin.

Jane Henschel and Luana Devol confirm their positions as leading Ammes and Färberins of their generation, and Susan Anthony is a richly ethereal Kaiserin: her farewell to the Amme and subsequent confrontation with the Hüter der Schwelle (Vater bist du's?) is heartrending, and reminds us that we already have here an accomplished Salome and Ariadne.

performance no 47

kaiserin	**silvana dussmann**
färberin	**elizabeth connell**
amme	**julia juon**
kaiser	**stuart skelton**
barak	**terje stensvold**
geisterbote	**simon bailey**
stimme des falken	**julia raschke**
erscheinung eines jünglings	**andreas herrmann**
hüter der schwelle	**julia raschke**
stimme von oben	**mora stettner**
der einäugige	**franz mayer**
der einarmige	**yan-lei chen**
der bucklige	**hans jürgen lazar**

performance no 47

date	17 february 2005/public performance
venue	oper frankfurt
orchestra	opern- und museumsorchester frankfurt
choirs	chor der oper frankfurt
conductor	**sebastian weigle**
comments	

Good quality in-house recording captures a rounded and polished performance. Outstanding the Färberpaar of Terje Stensvold and Elizabeth Connell.

kaiserin	**emily magee**
färberin	**lisa gasteen**
amme	**gabriele schnaut**
kaiser	**stuart skelton**
barak	**daniel sumegi**
geisterbote	**jan buchwald**
stimme des falken	**irene bespalovalte**
erscheinung eines jünglings	**benjamin hulett**
hüter der schwelle	**christine karg**
stimme von oben	**ann-beth solvang**
der einäugige	**moritz gogg**
der einarmige	**wilhelm schwinghammer**
der bucklige	**jürgen sacher**

performance no 48

date	21 february 2007/public performance
venue	staatsoper hamburg
orchestra	philharmonisches staatsorchester
choirs	chor der staatsoper hamburg
conductor	**simone young**

comments

Very slow tempi and a tentative feel to the orchestral execution deprive this performance of much energy, and a low key cast does not help.

performance no 49

kaiserin	**kirsten blanck**
färberin	**caroline whisnant**
amme	**wilja ernst-masuraitis**
kaiser	**lance ryan**
barak	**marcus jupither**
geisterbote	**edward gaunt**
stimme des falken	**daniela köhler**
erscheinung eines jünglings	**manuel kull**
hüter der schwelle	**daniela köhler**
stimme von oben	**julia oesch**
der einäugige	**armin kolarczyk**
der einarmige	**luiz molz**
der bucklige	**mathias wohlbrecht**

performance no 49

date	27 october 2007/public performance
venue	badisches staatstheater karlsruhe
orchestra	badische staatskapelle
choirs	badisches staatschor
conductor	**anthony bramall**

comments

This version shows that the provincial theatre whose recorded Ring cycle was the first to appear on budget-priced cd is still not lacking in enterprise in attempting to stage the Frau. That said, however, the results on this in-house tape are not impressive.

The major roles require singing personalities which they do not get here. Best of the bunch is Canadian tenor Lance Ryan as Kaiser, who has subsequently gone on to make his mark elsewhere.

The local audience is enthusiastic in its applause, but sadly Frosch will not survive merely as a repertory piece.

performance no 50

kaiserin	**eva marton**
färberin	**marilyn zschau**
amme	**brigitte fassbänder**
kaiser	**william johns**
barak	**alfred muff**
geisterbote	**hartmut welker**
stimme des falken	**gloria banditelli**
erscheinung eines jünglings	**lorio zennaro**
hüter der schwelle	**david knutson**
stimme von oben	**monica tagliasacchi**
der einäugige	**felice schiavi**
der einarmige	**giancarlo luccardi**
der bucklige	**francesco memeo**

performance no 50

date	6 march 1986/public peformance
venue	teatro alla scala milano
orchestra	orchestra del teatro alla scala
choirs	coro del teatro alla scala
conductor	**wolfgang sawallisch**

comments

A performance of incredible orchestral virtuosity, with the works's Wagnerian underlay permeated with Meditarranean transparency. Heaviest passages are highly animated, becoming a veritable kaleidoscope of brightly coloured detail.

Vocal dominance comes from the demonic Amme of Brigitte Fassbänder, and Marilyn Zschau is also a formidable Färberin. Only a squally Eva Marton lets the side down, rallying however for her Act 2 outbursts.

This is certainly one of the very best of the non-German editions, although the prompter is audible in the best Italian tradition!

performance no 51

kaiserin	**alessandra marc**
färberin	**sabine hass**
amme	**reinhild runkel**
kaiser	**gary lakes**
barak	**alan titus**
geisterbote	**albert dohmen**
stimme des falken	**anne schwanewilms**
erscheinung eines jünglings	**michael howard**
hüter der schwelle	**caterina beranova**
der einäugige	**will hartmann**
der einarmige	**albert dohmen**
der bucklige	**michael howard**

performance no 51

date	23 march 1996/public concert performance
venue	auditorio lingotto torino
orchestra	orchestra nazionale della rai
choirs	coro filarmonico di varsavia and piccoli cantori di torino
conductor	**giuseppe sinopoli**

comments

Presumably a trial run for the conductor prior to his Dresden performances and recording later in the same year (performance no 17).

Gary Lakes is a pleasing lyric voice rather than Heldentenor, whilst Alessandra Marc's distinctively haunting soprano portrays again an ideal Kaiserin.

Background hum on the recording suggests that it may have been taken down from television.

performance no 52

kaiserin	**inga nielsen**
färberin	**luana devol**
amme	**reinhild runkel**
kaiser	**jon frederic west**
barak	**alan titus**
geisterbote	**eike wilm schulte**
stimme des falken	**elena cassian**
erscheinung eines jünglings	**michael howard**
hüter der schwelle	**paola cigna**
stimme von oben	**sabrina de rose**
der einäugige	**jürgen schmeckenbecher**
der einarmige	**andreas macco**
der bucklige	**arnold bezuyen**

133
performance no 52

date   14 april 1999/public performance

venue   teatro alla scala milano

orchestra   orchestra del teatro alla scala

choirs   coro del teatro alla scala

conductor   **giuseppe sinopoli**

comments

This may be Sinopoli's finest extant performance of the Strauss score, vividly recorded and displaying an orchestral palette of subtelty and fine gradations. There are of course those, as far as this conductor is concerned, who find that momentum suffers from his dwelling on incidental detail, but I am not one of those critics.

An experienced cast is headed by a near ideal Färberpaar, Luana Devol and Alan Titus.

performance no 53

kaiserin	**adrianne pieczonka**
färberin	**elena pankratova**
amme	**lioba braun**
kaiser	**torsten kerl**
barak	**albert dohmen**
geisterbote	**samuel youn**
stimme des falken	**chen reiss**
erscheinung eines jünglings	**emanuele d'aguanno**
hüter der schwelle	**daniela schilacchi**
stimme von oben	**manuela bress**
der einäugige	**rolf haunstein**
der einarmige	**marcus hotlop**
der bucklige	**karl michael ebner**

135

performance no 53

date 29 april 2010/rehearsal performance

venue teatro communale firenze

orchestra orchestra del maggio musicale

choirs coro del maggio musicale

conductor **zubin mehta**

comments

Respectable run-through, recorded very close and therefore lacking in perspective.

The cast combines some experienced names with fresh-voiced newcomers but fails to reach a high level of inspiration.

performance no 54

kaiserin	**hildegard behrens**
färberin	**gwyneth jones**
amme	**mignon dunn**
kaiser	**rene kollo**
barak	**walter berry**
geisterbote	**franz grundheber**
stimme des falken	**elaine lublin**
erscheinung eines jünglings	**georges gautier**
hüter der schwelle	**helene garetti**
stimme von oben	**annick duterte**
der einäugige	**phillippe rouillon**
der einarmige	**jean-louis soumagnas**
der bucklige	**joachim arndt**

performance no 54

date	22 september 1980/televised public performance
venue	palais garnier paris
orchestra	orchestre de l'opera national
choirs	choeurs de l'opera national
conductor	**christoph von dohnanyi**
catalogue numbers	dvd: premiere opera DVD 5512/ encore DVD 2040

comments

This mediocre sound recording seems to have been made with hand-held microphone in front of a television receiver: I have sampled two different copies of that VHS videotape, both of which are both sonically and visually unacceptable.

As far as one can judge, Hildegard Behrens is a fine Kaiserin, whilst Rene Kollo as Kaiser sings with far greater commitment than one usually associates with him.

If a decent source could be found from which a re-mastering could be carried out, we might have a third official video recording of the opera to put beside those of Wolfgang Sawallisch and Georg Solti.

performance no 55

kaiserin	**gwyneth jones**/*for hildegard behrens*
färberin	**gwyneth jones**
amme	**reinhild runkel**
kaiser	**hermann winkler**
barak	**gerd feldhoff**
geisterbote	**roland hermann**
stimme des falken	**anne marie robinson**
erscheinung eines jünglings	**richard decker**
hüter der schwelle	**anne marie robinson**
stimme von oben	**anne gjevang**
der einäugige	**horst hiestermann**
der einarmige	**rudolf hartmann**
der bucklige	**werner gröschel**

performance no 55

date	24 november 1985/public performance
venue	opernhaus zürich
orchestra	orchester der oper zürich
choirs	chor der oper zürich
conductor	**ralf weikert**

comments

The idea of the personalities of Kaiserin and Färberin being two sides of the same persona, as with Elisabeth and Venus in Wagner's Tannhäuser, is an interesting one: it came close to realisation in this Zürich performance. Due to a last-minute indisposition by Hildegard Behrens, Gwyneth Jones consented to save the evening from cancellation by undertaking both her usual role of Färberin and that of Kaiserin. With judicious use of a "double" at certain junctures as well as in the final scene, this proved to be viable.

Jones's beautiful rendition of the scena "Vater bist du's?" in Act 3 more than rewards the listener's perseverance with in-house sound which is not of the utmost fidelity.

performance no 56

kaiserin	**ellen shade**
färberin	**deborah polaski**
amme	**reinhild runkel**
kaiser	**thomas moser**
barak	**wolfgang schöne**
geisterbote	**kristinn sigmundsson**
stimme des falken	**jeannette fischer**
erscheinung eines jünglings	**claude guyat**
hüter der schwelle	**jeannette fischer**
stimme von oben	**reinhild runkel**
der einäugige	**hans peter kammerer**
der einarmige	**andreas kohn**
der bucklige	**doug jones**

performance no 56

date	8 november 1992/public performance
venue	grand theatre geneve
orchestra	orchestre de la suisse romande
choirs	choeurs du grand theatre de geneve
conductor	**horst stein**
comments	

This high quality radio transmission is led in the best Kapellmeister tradition by Horst Stein: tempi are moderate but flexible throughout.

Little-known American soprano Ellen Shade sings a creditable Kaiserin, and Deborah Polasaki, still in fresh voice and just prior to her Bayreuth Brünnhilde, convinces as Färberin.

performance no 57

kaiserin	**luana devol**
färberin	**sabine hass**
amme	**anja silja**
kaiser	**thomas moser**
barak	**jean-philippe lafont**
geisterbote	**kristinn sigmundsson**
stimme des falken	**jeanette fischer**
erscheinung eines jünglings	**gregg fedderly**
hüter der schwelle	**jeanette fischer**
stimme von oben	**francois martinhead**
der einäugige	**jochen schmeckenbecher**
der einarmige	**thierry felix**
der bucklige	**adrian martin**

143

performance no 57

date 20 march 1994/public performance

venue theatre du chatelet paris

orchestra philharmonia orchestra london

conductor **christoph von dohnanyi**

comments

Performed in Paris as part of a regular residency there by London's Philharmonia Orchestra, this recalls their own high quality concert performances of opera during the earlier Walter Legge era, as well as its participation in many classic opera recordings from the Furtwängler Tristan onwards.

Despite misgivings about this conductor which I have expressed elsewhere, it is thrilling to hear him give the Philharmonia its head in the many climactic orchestral transitions which are a hallmark of Strauss's score.

Much anticipated here was the Amme of that great singing actress Anja Silja. Her fans have always overlooked the occasional squally tone as a worthwhile price to pay for such an overwhelming degree of dramatic commitment. As a native German speaker, she sings off the text in a way that few foreigners can really equal. Aided in the pit by ex-husband Dohnanyi, Silja's portrayal fully explores the tortured soul of the Amme.

performance no 58

kaiserin	**anna tomova-sintow**
färberin	**gwyneth jones**
amme	**reinhild runkel**
kaiser	**horst hoffmann**
barak	**jean-philippe lafont**
geisterbote	**malcolm rivers**
stimme des falken	**brigitte anselmino**
erscheinung eines jünglings	**alain gabriel**
hüter der schwelle	**artur stefanowicz**
stimme von oben	**nathalie stutzmann**
der einäugige	**philippe fourcade**
der einarmige	**chris de moor**
der bucklige	**ivan matiakj**

performance no 58

date 22 october 1995/public performance

venue opera de marseille

orchestra orchestre du theatre de marseille

choirs choeurs du theatre de marseille

conductor **friedrich pleyer**

catalogue numbers dvd: premiere opera DVD 5316

comments

Modest quality in-house recording, but sadly the voices are too close for comfortable listening, not least the characteristically overpowering Dame Gwyneth ! (my comment refers to the sound recording and not the video edition)

performance no 59

kaiserin	**ricarda merbeth**
färberin	**janice baird**
amme	**doris soffel**
kaiser	**robert dean smith**
barak	**andrew schroeder**
geisterbote	**samuel youn**
stimme des falken	**silvia weiss**
erscheinung eines jünglings	**martin mühle**
hüter der schwelle	**silvia weiss**
stimme von oben	**qiu lin zhang**
der einäugige	**hans-peter schneider**
der einarmige	**gregory reinhart**
der bucklige	**ricardo cassinelli**

performance no 59

date	6 october 2006/public performance
venue	theatre du capitole de toulouse
orchestra	orchestre du capitole de toulouse
choirs	choeurs du capitole de toulouse
conductor	**pinchas steinberg**
catalogue numbers	cd: private edition vienna

comments

This excellent sounding broadcast houses a less than distinguished performance, bland and uneventful or, as we might say, going through the motions. Maybe those who are sceptical about the work's performing traditions will find it refreshing to have it stripped of its basic sentiments in this way?

Ricarda Merbeth shows her Viennese origins and displays the strong influence of Leonie Rysanek in the part of Kaiserin.

performance no 60

kaiserin	**eva maria westbroek**
färberin	**christine brewer**
amme	**jane henschel**
kaiser	**jon villars**
barak	**franz hawlata**
geisterbote	**ralf lukas**
stimme des falken	**elena tsallagova**
erscheinung eines jünglings	**ryan macpherson**
hüter der schwelle	**elena tsallagova**
stimme von oben	**jane henschel**
der einäugige	**yuri kissin**
der einarmige	**gregory reinhart**
der bucklige	**john esterlin**

performance no 60

date	3 february 2008/public performance
venue	opera bastille paris
orchestra	orchestre de l'opera bastille
choirs	choeurs de l'opera bastille
conductor	**gustav kuhn**

comments

An in-house recording of average quality reveals orchestral playing of high accomplishment, even if the voices are balanced less prominently than one would ideally wish.

Christine Brewer is a noble Färberin, the other principals less outstanding but passable in their different roles.

Conductor Gustav Kuhn belies his unconventional reputation with a highly commanding presence and sweep.

performance no 61

kaiserin	**emily magee**
färberin	**janice baird**
amme	**birgit remmert**
kaiser	**roberto sacca**
barak	**michael volle**
geisterbote	**reinhard mayr**
stimme des falken	**sandra trattnig**
erscheinung eines jünglings	**peter sonn**
hüter der schwelle	**sandra trattnig**
stimme von oben	**wiebke lehmkuhl**
der einäugige	**valery murga**
der einarmige	**andreas hörl**
der bucklige	**martin zysse**

performance no 61

date	19 december 2009/public performance
venue	opernhaus zürich
orchestra	orchester der oper zürich
choirs	chor der oper zürich
conductor	**franz welser-möst**
comments	

An in-house recording of reasonably sophisticated quality, finely conducted but with a cast lacking in any special individuality.

performance no 62

kaiserin	**hildegard hillebrecht**
färberin	**inge borkh**
amme	**regina resnik**
kaiser	**james king**
barak	**donald mcintyre**
geisterbote	**forbes robinson**
stimme des falken	**maria pellegrini**
erscheinung eines jünglings	**jean bonhomme**
hüter der schwelle	**rhonda bruce**
stimme von oben	**elizabeth bainbridge**
der einäugige	**napoleon bisson**
der einarmige	**otakar kraus**
der bucklige	**david lennox**

performance no 62

date	17 june 1967/public performance
venue	royal opera house covent garden london
orchestra	orchestra of the royal opera house
choirs	chorus of the royal opera house
conductor	**georg solti**
catalogue numbers	cd: private edition vienna/house of opera CDBB 572/handelman 01893/ live opera heaven C 3166

comments

The first Covent Garden production of the opera was a pioneering venture and has some of the negative qualities associated with that.

Apart from odd moments of relaxation, the conducting is excitable and sometimes bombastic, and the German diction of the non-German speaking members of the cast leaves a lot to be desired.

Inge Borkh's impressive Färberin carries the performance. Hildegard Hillebrecht as Kaiserin has a certain cool quality, but it is clear why she was most people's unfavourite exponent of the German lyric repertoire during her short period of international exposure, with a tendency to squalliness when under any sort of pressure. Donald McIntyre's conscientious Barak is very much a work in progress, and although Regina Resnik may have the measure of the Amme, she really sounds more like Verdi's Mistress Quickly !

performance no 63

kaiserin	**heather harper**
färberin	**helga dernesch**
amme	**ruth hesse**
kaiser	**james king**
barak	**walter berry**
geisterbote	**forbes robinson**
stimme des falken	**eiddwen harrhy**
erscheinung eines jünglings	**robert tear**
hüter der schwelle	**teresa cahill**
stimme von oben	**patricia payne**
der einäugige	**william elvin**
der einarmige	**raimund herincx**
der bucklige	**paul crook**

performance no 63

date	5 april 1976/public performance
venue	royal opera house covent garden london
orchestra	orchestra of the royal opera house
choirs	chorus of the royal opera house
conductor	**georg solti**
catalogue numbers	cd: opera depot OD 10352/ fiori F 11023

comments

Whilst I recall that each revival of the Royal Opera's Frau was eagerly awaited and critically acclaimed, in retrospect and on the recorded evidence they lacked subtelty and Innigkeit, emphasising only the score's bright colours and melodramatic aspects.

Walter Berry was making a belated Covent Garden debut in the part of Barak, and there was in my view a very fine Kaiserin from Heather Harper, although critic Alan Blyth found that she "lacked the thrilling upper extension to make the character's tormented decisions truly soul-searing".

performance no 64

kaiserin	**anne evans**
färberin	**pauline tinsley**
amme	**patricia payne**
kaiser	**matti kastu**
barak	**norman bailey**
geisterbote	**geoffrey moses**
stimme des falken	**rita cullis**
erscheinung eines jünglings	**philip amos**
hüter der schwelle	**helen field**
stimme von oben	**catherine savory**
der einäugige	**arthur davies**
der einarmige	**russell smythe**
der bucklige	**julian moyle**

performance no 64

date	14 march 1981/public performance
venue	dominion theatre london
orchestra	orchestra of welsh national opera
choirs	chorus of welsh national opera
conductor	**richard armstrong**
catalogue numbers	cd: oriel music OMS 035/premiere opera 2351/handelman 02413

comments

This BBC recording of the highly successful English language version by Welsh National Opera must surely be a candidate for commercial issue in the Chandos CD series of operas in English. It represents the indigenous performance tradition at its very best, abetted by the accomplished playing of WNO's orchestra under Richard Armstrong.

In Anne Evans and Pauline Tinsley WNO boasted two dramatic singers of world class, equal in my view to any in the work's recorded history (at the time, both were fresh from their success in the company's famed Elektra production). Tinsley's desperation here found a perfect match in the noble humanity of Norman Bailey's Barak – their Act 3 duet must be one of the most heartrending in all the recordings, possibly only equalled by the Ludwig-Berry partnership.

All speaks very highly for WNO's musical preparation staff at a time when opera was still governed by important values like diction and fidelity to the dramaturgy. This was of course just before the craze for extreme productions started to take hold.

performance no 65

kaiserin	**ruth falcon**
färberin	**gwyneth jones**
amme	**helga dernesch**
kaiser	**robert schunk**
barak	**siegmund nimsgern**
geisterbote	**philip joll**
stimme des falken	**linda kitchen**
erscheinung eines jünglings	**keith howes**
hüter der schwelle	**judith howarth**
stimme von oben	**judith howarth**
der einäugige	**paul crook**
der einarmige	**eric garrett**
der bucklige	**anthony smith**

performance no 65

date	30 june 1987/public performance
venue	royal opera house covent garden
orchestra	orchestra of the royal opera house
choirs	chorus of the royal opera house
conductor	**christoph von dohnanyi**
comments	

Sonically this is the weakest of the recordings to derive from Covent Garden, with very distant balances.

The major cast members are all to be heard to better advantage in their roles at other venues.

performance no 66

kaiserin	**anna tomova-sintow**
färberin	**gwyneth jones**
amme	**jane henschel**
kaiser	**paul frey**
barak	**franz grundheber**
geisterbote	**robert haywood**
stimme des falken	**jacqueline fugella**
erscheinung eines jünglings	**albert janelli**
hüter der schwelle	**judith howarth**
stimme von oben	**gillian knight**
der einäugige	**daniel washington**
der einarmige	**roderick earle**
der bucklige	**anthony roden**

performance no 66

date	23 november 1992/public performances
venue	royal opera house covent garden london
orchestra	orchestra of the royal opera house
choirs	chorus of the royal opera house
conductor	**bernard haitink**
comments	

Haitink conducts a well-mannered and, for me, less interesting account of the score, with only Gwyneth Jones overstepping the bounds of politeness and giving her typically wild and manic portrayal of the Färberin.

This BBC broadcast was from the first run of the Royal Opera's second production of the opera. It attracted attention primarily through the stage designs by David Hockney (elsewhere Hockney had already designed Tristan and Zauberflöte).

performance no 67

kaiserin	**alessandra marc**
färberin	**johanna meier**
amme	**reinhild runkel**
kaiser	**james king**
barak	**franz grundheber**
geisterbote	**kristinn sigmundsson**
stimme des falken	**saskia gerritsen**
erscheinung eines jünglings	**alexander stevenson**
hüter der schwelle	**saskia gerritsen**
stimme von oben	**joke de vin**
der einäugige	**kristinn sigmundsson**
der einarmige	**lieuwe visser**
der bucklige	**alexander stevenson**

performance no 67

date	9 june 1990/public concert performance as part of the holland festival
venue	concertgebouw amsterdam
orchestra	radio philharmonisch orkest
choirs	groet omroepkoor and st bavo choir
conductor	**edo de waart**

comments

A valuable document, preserving what seems to be the work's first performance in the Netherlands.

The opera is symphonically paced by Edo de Waart in the full and ambient acoustic of the Concergebouw, with much loving attention to detail.

Veteran James King is still authoritative as Kaiser, with Johanna Meier a youthful Färberin in the mould of Christa Ludwig. Alessandra Marc is impetuous and ultra feminine as Kaiserin, with Reinhild Runkel giving a far more committed Amme than in the Solti recording from a year earlier.

performance no 68

kaiserin	**gabriele fontana**
färberin	**evelyn herlitzius**
amme	**doris soffel**
kaiser	**klaus florian vogt**
barak	**terje stensvold**
geisterbote	**petris egilitis**
stimme des falken	**lenneke ruiten**
erscheinung eines jünglings	**jean-leon klostermann**
hüter der schwelle	**lenneke ruiten**
stimme von oben	**corinne romijn**
der einäugige	**roger smeets**
der einarmige	**alexander vassiliev**
der bucklige	**torsten hofmann**

performance no 68

date	20 september 2008/public performance
venue	het musiektheater amsterdam
orchestra	nederlands philharmonisch orkest
choirs	chorus of nederlandse opera
conductor	**marc albrecht**
comments	

High quality Netherlands Radio recording of a fine performance led by Marc Albrecht, who seems to be emerging as the next leading German conductor after Christian Thielemann.

Klaus Florian Vogt must be the most mellifluous interpreter of Kaiser since Franz Völker, whilst Doris Soffel impresses as Amme. Gabriele Fontana is a more mature sounding Kaiserin, but Evelyn Herlitzius and Terje Stensvold are a well-matched Färberpaar, with inherent nobility under their long-suffering and tempetuous exteriors.

It is clear why Netherlands Philharmonic Orchestra is chosen by Netherlands Opera for so many of its productions, with its sensitive but committed playing in the pit.

performance no 69

kaiserin	**marion ammann**
färberin	**kirsi tilhonen**
amme	**julia juon**
kaiser	**john treleaven**
barak	**jukka rasilainen**
geisterbote	**sauli tilikainen**
stimme des falken	**sirkka lampimäki**
erscheinung eines jünglings	**petrus schroderus**
hüter der schwelle	**minttu pesu**
der einäugige	**hannu forsberg**
der einarmige	**peter lindroos**
der bucklige	**aki alamikkotervo**

performance no 69

date	6 february 2006/public performance
venue	finnish national opera helsinki
orchestra	finnish national orchestra
choirs	chorus of finnish national opera
conductor	**muhai tang**

comments

Flawless recording of an almost flawless performance and a remarkable achievement for a non-German company, with miraculously transparent orchestral playing.

Chinese conductor Muhai Tang leads a cast who have obviously immersed themselves in the work over a long and intensive rehearsal period.

The sole company guest is Heldentenor John Treleaven, who as Kaiser brings his customary hearty commitment to the role.

performance no 70

kaiserin	**leonie rysanek**
färberin	**marianne schech**
amme	**irene dalis**
kaiser	**ticho parly**
barak	**paul schöffler**
geisterbote	**robert anderson**
stimme des falken	**frances mccann**
erscheinung eines jünglings	**gilbert russell**
hüter der schwelle	**mary costa**
stimme von oben	**virginia starr**
der einäugige	**richard wentworth**
der einarmige	**lorenzo alvary**
der bucklige	**raymond manton**

performance no 70

date	24 september 1960/public performance
venue	war memorial opera house san francisco
orchestra	orchestra of san francisco opera
choirs	chorus of san francisco opera
conductor	**leopold ludwig**
comments	

A full one third of the opera is missing from this dim quality copy of the opera's North American premiere – only Act 3 is heard complete. However, as an important historical document it has at least to be considered.

The team of Marianne Schech and Paul Schöffler can be heard to be working well together, and Leonie Rysanek shines as she was to do later in the various New York recordings.

performance no 71

kaiserin	**ingrid bjoner**
färberin	**gladys kuchta**
amme	**grace hofmann**
kaiser	**sebastian feiersinger**
barak	**mino yahia**
geisterbote	**hans gunter nöcker**
stimme des falken	**susanna rouco**
erscheinung eines jünglings	**eduardo sarramidai**
hüter der schwelle	**olga chevaline retes**
stimme von oben	**marilu anselmi**
der einäugige	**gianpiero mastromei**
der einarmige	**f. linke**
der bucklige	**jose naiti**

171
performance no 71

date	10 october 1965/public performance
venue	teatro colon buenos aires
orchestra	orquesta del teatro colon
choirs	coro del teatro colon
conductor	**ferdinand leitner**

comments

A good quality in-house recording gives us a good idea of this underrated conductor's operatic work.

Real Heldentenor timbre adds weight to Feiersinger's Kaiser. This version is also valuable for giving us another chance to appreciate the accomplished Färberin of Gladys Kuchta.

performance no 72

kaiserin	**leonie rysanek**
färberin	**christa ludwig**
amme	**irene dalis**
kaiser	**james king**
barak	**walter berry**
geisterbote	**william dooley**
stimme des falken	**carlotta ordassy**
erscheinung eines jünglings	**robert nagy**
hüter der schwelle	**mary ellen pracht**
stimme von oben	**helen amparan**
der einäugige	**clifford harvuot**
der einarmige	**lorenzo alvary**
der bucklige	**paul franke**

performance no 72

date	17 december 1966/public performance
venue	metropolitan opera house new york
orchestra	orchestra of the metropolitan opera
choirs	chorus of the metropolitan opera
conductor	**karl böhm**
catalogue numbers	cd: omega opera archive OOA 1124/ LYR 14/opera lovers FRAU 196601

comments

This Met broadcast from the opening season in their new house comes complete with the radio announcements.

On sonic terms alone it is clear why these performances should have stolen the limelight from Barber's Antony and Cleopatra. Leonie Rysanek is at her peak (when was she not?), as is Christa Ludwig.

Böhm's contribution is a marvel of taut and purposeful conducting, ideal for convincing a reluctant New York public of the work's merits.

performance no 73

kaiserin	**leonie rysanek**
färberin	**christa ludwig**
amme	**irene dalis**
kaiser	**james king**
barak	**walter berry**
geisterbote	**william dooley**
stimme des falken	**carlotta ordassy**
erscheinung eines jünglings	**robert nagy**
hüter der schwelle	**mary ellen pracht**
stimme von oben	**batyah godfrey ben-david**
der einäugige	**theodore lambrinos**
der einarmige	**lorenzo alvary**
der bucklige	**paul franke**

performance no 73

date	8 march 1969/public performance
venue	metopolitan opera house new york
orchestra	orchestra of the metropolitan opera
choirs	chorus of the metropolitan opera
conductor	**karl böhm** |//

comments

The same comments apply as for performance no 72, which had identical principals for this revival.

performance no 74

kaiserin	**ingrid bjoner**
färberin	**daniza mastilovic**
amme	**grace hofmann**
kaiser	**waldemar kmentt**
barak	**donald mcintyre**
geisterbote	**angelo mattiello**
stimme des falken	**cristina carlin**
erscheinung eines jünglings	**jose naiti**
hüter der schwelle	**africa de retes**
stimme von oben	**isabel casey**
der einäugige	**ricardo yost**
der einarmige	**jorge algorta**
der bucklige	**eugenio valoni**

performance no 74

date 13 october 1970/public performance

venue teatro colon buenos aires

orchestra orquesta del teatro colon

choirs coro del teatro colon

conductor **ferdinand leitner**

comments

The potential interest of this version would be Waldemar Kmentt, the Viennese tenor who did not take the role of Kaiser elsewhere (at his home base he sang one solitary performance as the Jüngling).

Sadly the sound quality, presumably several genertions removed from the original radio broadcast, allows little investigation of the performance's merits.

performance no 75

kaiserin	**leonie rysanek**
färberin	**christa ludwig**
amme	**irene dalis**
kaiser	**robert nagy**
barak	**walter berry**
geisterbote	**william dooley**
stimme des falken	**carlotta ordassy**
erscheinung eines jünglings	**rod macwherter**
hüter der schwelle	**mary ellen pracht**
stimme von oben	**batyah godfrey ben-david**
der einäugige	**clifford harvuot**
der einarmige	**lorenzo alvary**
der bucklige	**paul franke**

performance no 75

date	16 january 1971/public performance
venue	metropolitan opera house new york
orchestra	orchestra of the metropolitan opera
choirs	chorus of the metropolitan opera
conductor	**karl böhm**
catalogue numbers	cd: private edition vienna

comments

Böhm's pioneering Metropolitan Opera performances, starting at the 1966 re-opening of the new house, are well documented, with this one perhaps the pick of the bunch. It is the last of three official Met broadcasts of the series, with only the regular Kaiser of James King being replaced by Robert Nagy.

The Färberpaar of Christa Ludwig-Walter Berry are at their dramatic peak, giving remarkably moving portrayals when one considers that their real-life marriage had recently come to an end. Ludwig in particular is absolutely fearless in her Act 2 outbursts. Irene Dalis delivers a truly malevolent Amme, which I had previously encountered in a Hamburg State Opera performance which had been London's first exposure to the work in 1966 (guest performances at the Sadlers Wells Theatre).

Standard cuts notwithstanding, the Met orchestra responds to Böhm's authoritative direction with playing of a virtuoso calibre.

performance no 76

kaiserin	**leonie rysanek**
färberin	**inge borkh**
amme	**irene dalis**
kaiser	**robert nagy**
barak	**walter berry**
geisterbote	**william dooley**
stimme des falken	**carlotta ordassy**
erscheinung eines jünglings	**rod macwherter**
hüter der schwelle	**joy clements**
stimme von oben	**batyah godfrey ben-david**
der einäugige	**clifford harvuot**
der einarmige	**lorenzo alvary**
der bucklige	**paul franke**

181

performance no 76

date 11 february 1971/public performance

venue metropolitan opera house new york

orchestra orchestra of the metropolitan opera

choirs chorus of the metropolitan opera

conductor **karl böhm**

comments

An in-house recording with intrusive audience noises, it showcases Leonie Rysanek at her thrilling best in her signature role as well as high-level contributions from Robert Nagy as Kaiser and Inge Borkh, now replacing Christa Ludwig as Färberin.

This version is also worth sampling for the loving care which conductor Böhm lavishes on the orchestral interludes.

performance no 77

kaiserin	**leonie rysanek**
färberin	**ursula schröder-feinen**
amme	**ruth hesse**
kaiser	**matti kastu**
barak	**walter berry**
geisterbote	**james johnson**
stimme des falken	**linda roark-strummer**
erscheinung eines jünglings	**james hobeck**
hüter der schwelle	**claudia cummings**
stimme von oben	**gwendolyn jones**
der einäugige	**joshua hecht**
der einarmige	**lorenzo alvary**
der bucklige	**john duykkers**

performancce no 77

date	15 october 1976/public performance
venue	war memorial opera house san francisco
orchestra	orchestra of san francisco opera
choirs	chorus of san francisco opera
conductor	**karl böhm**
catalogue numbers	cd: san francisco opera SFO 03/ audio encyclopedia AE 201B

comments

This is a professional quality recording from KKH1/SF radio station of the first night of a new production in the very house where, sixteen years earlier, the opera had received its North American premiere (performance no 70).

It was also Böhm's first operatic appearance in an American theatre other than the Metropolitan, for which he brought with him (with one exception) the principals from his Salzburg performances in 1974-1976. Indeed, Met-based bass Lorenzo Alvary had been a constant as the one-armed brother in Böhm's presentations both in New York and Salzburg.

The high-fidelity sound, complete with tasteful broadcast announcements (in contrast to those at the Met), gives a very forward balance to the voices, especially to Ursula Schröder-Feinen at her clarion best as Färberin.

performance no 78

kaiserin	**leonie rysanek**
färberin	**ursula schröder-feinen**
amme	**mignon dunn**
kaiser	**james king**
barak	**walter berry**
geisterbote	**vern shinell**
stimme des falken	**louise wohlafka**
erscheinung eines jünglings	**john carpenter**
hüter der schwelle	**loretta di franco**
stimme von oben	**batyah godfrey ben-david**
der einäugige	**russell christopher**
der einarmige	**lorenzo alvary**
der bucklige	**paul franke**

performance no 78

date	1 april 1978/public performance
venue	metropolitan opera house new york
orchestra	orchestra of the metropolitan opera
choirs	chorus of the metropolitan opera
conductor	**karl böhm**
catalogue numbers	cd: LYR 22

comments

This Met broadcast is from Böhm's last season of conducting at the house, and displays all of the virtues which were a constant of his performances.

It is also the last time that this opera was given in New York in the standard cut vesion. The next revival (performance no 81) would see an early attempt to open up all those cuts.

performance no 79

kaiserin	**eva marton**
färberin	**birgit nilsson**
amme	**ruth hesse**
kaiser	**jess thomas**
barak	**siegmund nimsgern**
geisterbote	**levon boghossian**
stimme des falken	**maria farre**
erscheinung eines jünglings	**dante ranieri**
hüter der schwelle	**africa de retes**
stimme von oben	**marilu anselmi**
der einäugige	**mario solomonoff**
der einarmige	**jorge algorta**
der bucklige	**ricardo cassinelli**

performance no 79

date	14 october 1979/public performance
venue	teatro colon buenos aires
orchestra	orquesta del teatro colon
choirs	coro del teatro colon
cnductor	**marek janowski**

comments

A closely miked radio broadcast which spotlights the orchestral contribution but also the indistinct diction of many minor roles and the unwelcome prominence of the prompter.

The cast of principals I would describe as of average quality.

performance no 80

kaiserin	**leonie rysanek**
färberin	**birgit nilsson**
amme	**ruth hesse**
kaiser	**james king**
barak	**gerd feldhoff**
geisterbote	**raimund herincx**
stimme des falken	**rebecca cook**
erscheinung eines jünglings	**james hoback**
hüter der schwelle	**pamela smith**
stimme von oben	**gwendolyn jones**
der einäugige	**john del carlo**
der einarmige	**arnold voketailis**
der bucklige	**michael ballam**

performance no 80

date	30 september 1980/public performance
venue	war memorial opera house san francisco
orchestra	orchestra of the san francisco opera
choirs	chorus of the san francisco opera
conductor	**berislav klobubar**
catalogue numbers	cd: premiere opera CDN 03188

comments

Another Kapellmeeister of the old school, Berislav Klobucar leads a steadily paced performance in good quality broadcast sound.

In the cast of European principals familiar with their roles over many years, Birgit Nilsson again fails to convince me of her rightness for the part of Färberin (too much steely brilliance?), whilst Ruth Hesse is an instance of a singer taking her role too often: she is much afflicted by the wobble which I also recall from her Fricka and Ortrud.

performance no 81

kaiserin	**eva marton**
färberin	**birgit nilsson**
amme	**mignon dunn**
kaiser	**gerd brenneis**
barak	**franz ferdinand nentwig**
geisterbote	**franz mazura**
stimme des falken	**louise wohlafka**
erscheinung eines jünglings	**timothy jenkins**
hüter der schwelle	**eleanor bergquist**
stimme von oben	**batyah godfrey ben-david**
der einäugige	**russell christopher**
der einarmige	**james courtney**
der bucklige	**john gilmore**

performance no 81

date	23 october 1981/public performance
venue	metropolitan opera house new york
orchestra	orchestra of the metropolitan opera
choirs	chorus of the metropolitan opera
conductor	**erich leinsdorf**
catalogue numbers	cd: LYR 58

comments

Much vaunted for the restoration of cuts, Leinsdorf's conducting is nonetheless lacking in seduction, and the work's seriousness is not brought out by some funereal tempi. At best, the performance is analytical in its clarity.

In general this is a less distinguished cast that the one to which the Met had become accustomed during the Böhm era.

A second in-house recording from the run of performances conducted by Erich Leinsdorf is reported to be in circulation, but I have not been able to locate it.

performance no 82

kaiserin	**eva marton**
färberin	**marilyn zschau**
amme	**mignon dunn**
kaiser	**william johns**
barak	**siegmund nimsgern**
geisterbote	**michael devlin**
stimme des falken	**sandra moon**
erscheinung eines jünglings	**gregory kunde**
hüter der schwelle	**sandra moon**
stimme von oben	**gwyneth bean**
der einäugige	**dan sullivan**
der einarmige	**arnold voketailis**
der bucklige	**richard versalle**

193

performance no 82

date	19 november 1984/public performance
venue	lyric opera house chicago
orchestra	orchestra of the chicago lyric opera
choirs	chorus of the chicago lyric opera
conductor	**marek janowski**
catalogue numbers	cd: premiere opera 02312

comments

This high quality radio transmission encases one of the very best of the unpublished editions of the piece.

A uniformly excellent cast (even Eva Marton's Kaiserin eclipses her other performances of the role) is accompanied idiomatically by a well-trained orchestral apparatus.

This could well be mistaken for the work of one of the leading European ensembles.

performance no 83

kaiserin	**johanna meier**
färberin	**janis martin**
amme	**helga dernesch**
kaiser	**robert schunk**
barak	**james courtney**
geisterbote	**franz mazura**
stimme des falken	**kaaren erickson**
erscheinung eines jünglings	**mark baker**
hüter der schwelle	**heidi grant murphy**
stimme von oben	**gwyneth bean**
der einäugige	**russell christopher**
der einarmige	**richard vernon**
der bucklige	**richard fracker**

performance no 83

date	9 december 1989/public performance
venue	metropolitan opera house new york
orchestra	orchestra of the metropolitan opera
choirs	chorus of the meropolitan opera
conductor	**christof prick**

comments

A fine-sounding Met broadcast with broad and sensitive direction from Maestro Prick (sometimes referred to outside the German-speaking world as Perick).

Many cuts are opened, but there is some weakness, in my view, from the male principals. Helga Dernesch may have been more suited to her previous part as Färberin, although that role is taken here by the much under-appreciated American mezzo Janis Martin.

performance no 84

kaiserin	**mary jane johnson**
färberin	**gwyneth jones**
amme	**anja silja**
kaiser	**william johns**
barak	**alfred muff**
geisterbote	**monte pederson**
stimme des falken	**patricia racette**
erscheinung eines jünglings	**hong-shen li**
hüter der schwelle	**maria fortuna**
stimme von oben	**carla cook**
der einäugige	**philip skinner**
der einarmige	**victor ledbetter**
der bucklige	**john duykers**

197
performance no 84

date 10 december 1989/public performance

venue war memorial opera house san francisco

orchestra orchestra of the san francisco opera

choirs chorus of the san francisco opera

conductor **christoph von dohnanyi**

catalogue numbers cd: premiere opera 02337

comments

Rather remotely recorded in-house, this version gives only a pale impression of the musical happenings. Fortunately, at least some of the principals can be judged from performances on other occasions.

performance no 85

kaiserin	**deborah voigt**
färberin	**gabriele schnaut**
amme	**reinhild runkel**
kaiser	**thomas moser**
barak	**wolfgang brendel**
geisterbote	**eike wilm schulte**
stimme des falken	**julia faulkner**
erscheinung eines jünglings	**mark schowalter**
hüter der schwelle	**jennifer welch-babidge**
stimme von oben	**jane bunnell**
der einäugige	**timothy nolen**
der einarmige	**james courtney**
der bucklige	**allan glassman**

performance no 85

date   5 january 2002/public performance

venue   metropolitan opera house new york

orchestra   orchestra of the metropolitan opera

choirs   chorus of the metropolitan opera

conductor   **christian thielemann**

comments

Unfortuntely Thielemann's much anticipated series of mid-winter performances of the Strauss opera during the 2001-2002 season were beset by some unsettling cast changes in the course of the run.

Whilst Voigt is still fresh voice, both Runkel and Moser were below par.

However, this is a fine orchestral achievement even by the Met's consistently high standard of playing, and it is a matter of regret that the company has not subsequently sought to secure Christian Thielemann's services on at least a regular guest basis.

performance no 86

kaiserin	**deborah voigt**
färberin	**christine brewer**
amme	**michaela martens**
kaiser	**robert dean smith**
barak	**franz hawlata**
geisterbote	**quinn kelsey**
stimme des falken	**stacey tappan**
erscheinung eines jünglings	**bryan griffin**
hüter der schwelle	**stacey tappan**
stimme von oben	**meredith arwady**
der einäugige	**daniel sutin**
der einarmige	**andrew funk**
der bucklige	**john easterling**

performance no 86

date	30 november 2007/public performance
venue	lyric opera house chicago
orchestra	orchestra of the chicago lyric opera
choirs	chorus of the chicago lyric opera
conductor	**andrew davis**
catalogue numbers	cd: live opera heaven C 3170/ premiere opera 02982

comments

A good quality in-house tape lies at the basis of this remarkable rendering. Andrew Davis seems to be only the third British maestro ever to have conducted a new production of the Strauss work. The quality of the recorded result is not so surprising when one considers Davis's pedigree of Strauss opera appearances both at Covent Garden and Glyndebourne as well as more recently in his tenure at Chicago.

The Färberpaar of Christine Brewer and Franz Hawlata remain vocally unchallenged by other recent contenders in their parts – Brewer in particular is heroic and appealingly feminine at the same time. Deborah Voigt has certainly deepened her portrayal in the ten years since she first took on the role of Kaiserin, and is caught here before the ridiculous weight loss robbed her voice of its hochdramatisch status.

appendix a: recorded performances which have not been heard
this is because of inferior sound quality or simply non-availability of a copy. listing is chronological and not by country of origin, and information is given in the order of date, venue, conductor and the six principal roles (kaiserin/ färberin/ amme/ kaiser/ barak/ geisterbote)

performance no 87
25 october 1966/new york metropolitan/**karl böhm**
bjoner/ludwig/dalis/king/berry/dooley

performance no 88
17 february 1971/new york metropolitan/**karl böhm**
rysanek/borkh/dalis/nagy/berry/dooley

performance no 89
13 december 1975/stockholm/**berislav klobucar**
wennberg/nilsson/ericson/kastu/berry/lundborg

performance no 90
21 february 1976/stockholm/**berislav klobucar**
wennberg/nilsson/ericson/kastu/jupither/tyren

performance no 91
15 may 1977/frankfurt-am-main/**christoph von dohnanyi**
marton/mastilovic/paustian/cochran/constantin/de kanel

performance no 92
1977/düsseldorf/**günter wich**
behrens/schröder-feinen/kim/kastu/feldhoff

performance no 93
17 october 1978/karlsruhe/**christof prick**
hass/vinzing/kim/de ridder/rafell/kirchner
audio cassette: handelman 06862

performance no 94
january 1984/deutsche staatsoper berlin/**ernst märzendorfer**
tarres/dvorakova/trekel-burkhardt/goldberg/pallay/svorc

performance no 95
1 february 1984 or 21 july 1985/karlsruhe/**christof prick**
habereder/vinzing/trekel-burkhardt/hopferwieser/kiemer

performance no 96
15 march 1986/bayerische staatsoper/**wolfgang sawallisch**
marton/zschau/fassbänder/johns/muff/welker

performance no 97
23 february 1992/wiener staatsoper/**horst stein**
haubold/jones/runkel/schunk/weikl/wimberger

performance no 98
27 november 1994/zürich/**christoph von dohnanyi**
lechner/jones/silja/winbergh/muff/scharinger
cd: premiere 2303

performance no 99
february 1996/amsterdam/**hartmut haenchen**
shade/schnaut/henschel/moser/bröcheler
dvd: house of opera DVDC 581

performance no 100
17 june or 3 july 1997/geneva/**armin jordan**
huffstodt/balslev/denize/sylvester/van dam/schulte

performance no 101
3 october 1998/deutsche oper berlin/**christian thielemann**
voigt/marton/henschel/moser/titus/carlson

performance no 102
november 2000/barcelona/**peter schneider**
gierhardt/marton/schwarz/woodrow/schöne
vhs video: handelman 09408
dvd: premiere opera DVD 5354

performance no 103
25 december 2000/wiener staatsoper/**simone young**
anthony/polaski/henschel/botha/struckmann/bankl

performance no 104
15 february 2001/semperoper dresden/**giuseppe sinopoli**
studer/devol/schwarz/botha/titus/ketelsen

performance no 105
17 october 2001/covent garden/**christoph von dohnanyi**
voigt/schnaut/henschel/botha/titus/booth-jones

performance no 106
25 october 2001/covent garden/**christoph von dohnanyi**
voigt/schnaut/henschel/winslade/titus/booth-jones

performance no 107
11 january 2002/new york metropolitan/**christian thielemann**
patchell/schnaut/schwarz/horton murray/brendel/dworchak

performance no 108
11 october 2002/athens/**michael schonwandt**
nielsen/marton/zschau/hamilton/grundheber/lorenz
cd: premiere opera 906

performance no 109
18 november 2002/wiener staatsoper/**michael boder**
nielsen/devol/henschel/winslade/struckmann/daniel

performance no 110
9 or 18 december 2002/opera bastille/**ulf schirmer**
anthony/devol/henschel/moser/lafont/kristinsson
cd: premiere opera 943

performance no 111
24 october 2003/wiener staatsoper/**simone young**
anthony/schnaut/henschel/winslade/struckmann/sim

performance no 112
21 november 2003/new york metropolitan/**philippe auguin**
voigt/polaski/juon/horton murray/brendel/delavan

performance no 113
10 december 2003/new york metropolitan/**philippe auguin**
voigt/polaski/henschel/winslade/brendel/delavan

performance no 114
2 march 2004/los angeles/**kent nagano**
nielsen/watson/soffel/dean smith/brendel/cresswell

performance no 115
23 january 2005/deutsche oper berlin/**christian thielemann**
voigt/devol/henschel/winslade/grundheber/carlson

performance no 116
1 march 2005/semperoper dresden/**michael boder**
anthony/schnaut/szönyi/gould/rasilainen/ketelsen

performance no 117
7 or 11 june 2005/monnaie bruxelles/**kazuski ono**
dussmann/schnaut/schuster/villars/van dam/peeters
cd: premiere opera 1809/house of opera CDN 18093

performance no 118
11 september 2005/frankfurt-am-main/**johannes debus**
fontana/connell/juon/skelton/silins/eglitis

appendix b: officially published scenes or excerpts

act one: ist mein liebster dahin, was weckst du mich so früh?
eleanor steber (kaiserin)
edwin biltcliffe (pianist)
recorded on 10 october 1958 at a concert in new york
lp: private issue SLP 101
cd: vai audio VAIA 10052

deborah voigt (kaiserin)
sinfonieorchester des bayerischen rundfunks
richard armstrong
recorded between 22-26 september 2003 in the herkulessaal munich
cd: emi 557 6812

act one: sie aus dem hause!....aus einem jungen munde gehen harte worte
gisela schröter (färberin)
theo adam (barak)
sächsische staatskapelle dresden
otmar suitner
recorded between 6-10 january 1969 in the lukaskirche dresden
lp: eterna 826 097/827 407/telefunken SAT 22513
cd: berlin classics 13222/95152

act one: sinfonisches zwischenspiel
sächsische staatskapelle dresden
karl böhm
recorded in june 1942 by the reichsrundfunk in the semperoper dresden
lp: acanta DE 23280-23281

act one: sie haben es mir gesagt, dass ihre seele seltsam sein wird
josef herrmann (barak)
chor der staatsoper dresden
sächsische staatskapelle dresden
karl böhm
recorded in june 1942 by the reichsrundfunk in the semperoper dresden
lp: acanta 77221 792/DE 23108-23109/DE 23280-23281
cd: profil medien PH 07039

theo adam (barak)
chor der staatsoper dresden
sächsische staatskapelle dresden
otmar suitner
recorded between 6-10 january 1969 in the lukaskirche dresden
lp: eterna 826 097/827 407
cd: berlin classics 13222/95152

act two: falke du wiedergefundener!
torsten ralf (kaiser)
sächsische staatskapelle dresden
karl böhm
recorded in june 1942 by the reichsrundfunk in the semperoper dresden
lp: eterna 820 933/acanta DE 23280-23281
cd: berlin classics 20492/25002/93942/
preiser 89077/profil medien PH 07039

act two: wehe mein mann!
leontyne price (kaiserin)
patricia clark (stimme des falken)
ambrosian singers
new philharmonia orchestra
erich leinsdorf
recorded between 9-11 july 1973 in the town hall walthamstow
lp: victor ARL1-0333/TRL1-7044/CML 082
cd: rca/bmg GD 60398/GD 86672/
09026 681532
this version commences earlier at sieh des mannes aug'!

susan anthony (kaiserin)
slovak radio symphony orchestra
ivan anguelov
recorded between 14-18 may 2001 in the concert hall of slovak radio bratislava
cd: arte nova 74321 868942

deborah voigt (kaiserin)
sinfonieorchester des bayerischen rundfunks
richard armstrong
recorded between 22-26 september 2003 in the herkulessaal munich
cd: emi 557 6812

act three: schweigt doch ihr stimmen!.....barak mein mann!......mir anvertraut
iva pacetti (färberin)
benvenuto franci (barak)
orchestra del teatro alla scala
gino marinuzzi
recorded on 6 january 1940 at a performance in the teatro alla scala di milano
lp: fonit cetra documents DOC 25
cd: preiser 89124
this version is sung in italian

christa ludwig (färberin)
walter berry (barak)
sieglinde wagner (stimme von oben)
orchester der deutschen oper berlin
heinrich hollreiser
recorded in 1964 in berlin
lp: eurodisc 71187KR/27991CR/
world records CM 70/SCM 70
cd: rca/bmg 09026 689512/tessitura music 0049
this version commences only at barak mein mann!

christine brewer (färberin)
eric owens (barak)
atlanta symphony orchestra
donald runnicles
recorded in 2009 in atlanta
cd: telarc 31755

act three: vater bist du's?
eleanor steber (kaiserin)
edwin biltcliffe (pianist)
recorded on 10 october 1958 at a concert in new york
lp: private issue SLP 101
cd: vai audio VAIA 10052

list of discography subscribers

production of these discographies would not have been possible without the loyal support over many years of

Richard Ames
Yoshihiro Asada
J.M. Blyth
Marc Bridle
Robert Dandois
Richard Dennis
Hans Peter Ebner
Nobuo Fukumoto
Philip Goodman
Johann Gratz
Tadashi Hasegawa
Ernest Johnson
Koji Kinoshita
J-F. Lambert
John Mallinson
Carlo Marinelli
Bruce Morrison
Alan Newcombe
Hugh Palmer
David Patmore
J.A. Payne
Tully Potter
Yutaka Sasaki
Robert Simmons
Michael Tanner
Nigel Wood
Ken Wyman
Stefano Angeloni
Reinier van Bevorvoorde
Michael Brel
Brian Capon
Dennis Davis
John Derry
Martin Elste
Brian Godfrey
Jean-Pierre Goossens
Alan Haine
Naoya Hirabayashi
Rodney Kempster
Detlef Kissmann
Graham Lilley
Douglas McIntosh
Philip Moores
William Moyle
Gregory Page-Turner
Laurence Pateman
John Pattrick
James Pearson
Klaus Reuther
Ingo Schwarz
Yoshihiko Suzuki
Urs Weber
Graeme Wright

Books published by Travis & Emery Music Bookshop:
Anon.: Hymnarium Sarisburiense, cum Rubricis et Notis Musicis.
Anon.: Säcularfeier des Geburtstages von Ludwig van Beethoven
Agricola, Johann Friedrich from Tosi: Anleitung zur Singkunst.
Allen, Percy: The Stage Life of Mrs. Stirling: With ... C19th Theatre
Bach, C.P.E.: edited W. Emery: Nekrolog or Obituary Notice of J.S. Bach.
Bateson, Naomi Judith: Alcock of Salisbury
Bathe, William: A Briefe Introduction to the Skill of Song
Berlioz, Hector: Autobiography of Hector Berlioz, (2 vols.)
Buckley, Robert John: Sir Edward Elgar
Burney, Charles: The Present State of Music in France and Italy
Burney, Charles: The Present State of Music in Germany, The Netherlands ...
Burney, Charles: Account of an Infant Musician
Burney, Charles: An Account of the Musical Performances ... Handel
Burney, Karl: Nachricht von Georg Friedrich Handel's Lebensumstanden.
Burns, Robert: The Caledonian Musical Museum .. Best Scotch Songs. (1810)
Cobbett, W.W.: Cobbett's Cyclopedic Survey of Chamber Music. (2 vols.)
Corrette, Michel: Le Maitre de Clavecin
Cox, John Edmund: Musical Recollections of the Last Half Century. (2 vols.)
Crimp, Bryan: Dear Mr. Rosenthal ... Dear Mr. Gaisberg ...
Crimp, Bryan: Solo: The Biography of Solomon
Crotch, William: Substance of Several Courses of Lectures on Music
d'Indy, Vincent: Beethoven: Biographie Critique
d'Indy, Vincent: Beethoven: A Critical Biography
d'Indy, Vincent: Cesar Franck (in English)
d'Indy, Vincent: César Franck (in French)
Dianna, B.A.: Benjamin Britten's Holy Theatre
Dolge, Alfred: Pianos and Their Makers. A Comprehensive History
Fischhof, Joseph: Versuch einer Geschichte des Clavierbaues. (Faksimile 1853).
Fuller-Maitland, J.A.: The Music of Parry and Stanford
Geminiani, Francesco: The Art of Playing the Violin.
Häuser: Musikalisches Lexikon. 2 vols in one.
Hawkins, John: A General History of the Science & Practice of Music (5 vols.)
Herbert-Caesari, Edgar: The Science and Sensations of Vocal Tone
Herbert-Caesari, Edgar: Vocal Truth
Holmes, Edward: A Ramble among the Musicians of Germany
Hopkins, Antony: The Concertgoer's Companion - Bach to Haydn.
Hopkins, Antony: The Concertgoer's Companion – Holst to Webern.
Hopkins, Antony: Music All Around Me
Hopkins, Antony: Sounds of Music / Sounds of the Orchestra
Hopkins, Antony: The Nine Symphonies of Beethoven

Books published by Travis & Emery Music Bookshop:

Hopkins, Antony: Understanding Music
Hopkins, Edward & Rimboult, Edward: The Organ. Its History & Construction.
Hunt, John: - see separate list of discographies at the end of these titles
Iliffe, Frederick: The Forty-Eight Preludes and Fugues of John Sebastian Bach
Isaacs, Lewis: Hänsel and Gretel. A Guide to Humperdinck's Opera.
Isaacs, Lewis: Königskinder (Royal Children). Guide to Humperdinck's Opera.
Kastner: Manuel Général de Musique Militaire
Kenney, Charles Lamb: A Memoir of Michael William Balfe
Klein, Hermann: Thirty years of musical Life in London, 1870-1900
Lacassagne, M. l'Abbé Joseph : Traité Général des élémens du Chant
Lascelles (née Catley), Anne: The Life of Miss Anne Catley.
McCormack, John: John McCormack: His Own Life Story.
Mainwaring, John: Memoirs of the Life of the Late George Frederic Handel
Malcolm, Alexander: A Treaty of Music: Speculative, Practical and Historical
Marx, Adolph Bernhard: Die Kunst des Gesanges, Theoretisch-Practisch
May, Florence: The Life of Brahms
May, Florence: The Girlhood Of Clara Schumann: Clara Wieck And Her Time.
Mellers, Wilfrid: Angels of the Night: Popular Female Singers of Our Time
Mellers, Wilfrid: Bach and the Dance of God
Mellers, Wilfrid: Beethoven and the Voice of God
Mellers, Wilfrid: Caliban Reborn - Renewal in Twentieth Century Music
Mellers, Wilfrid: Darker Shade of Pale, A Backdrop to Bob Dylan
Mellers, Wilfrid: François Couperin and the French Classical Tradition
Mellers, Wilfrid: Harmonious Meeting
Mellers, Wilfrid: Le Jardin Retrouvé, The Music of Frederic Mompou
Mellers, Wilfrid: Music and Society, England and the European Tradition
Mellers, Wilfrid: Music in a New Found Land: … … American Music
Mellers, Wilfrid: Romanticism and the Twentieth Century (from 1800)
Mellers, Wilfrid: The Masks of Orpheus: …… the Story of European Music.
Mellers, Wilfrid: The Sonata Principle (from c. 1750)
Mellers, Wilfrid: Vaughan Williams and the Vision of Albion
Newmarch, Rosa: Henry J. Wood
Newmarch, Rosa: Jean Sibelius
Newmarch, Rosa: Mary Wakefield, a Memoir
Newmarch, Rosa: The Concert-Goer's Library
Newmarch, Rosa: The Music of Czechoslovakia.
Newmarch, Rosa: The Russian Opera.
Niecks, Frederick: The Life oc Chopin. (2 vols.)
Panchianio, Cattuffio: Rutzvanscad Il Giovine

Books published by Travis & Emery Music Bookshop:

Pearce, Charles: Sims Reeves, Fifty Years of Music in England.
Pepusch, John Christopher: A Treatise on Harmony ...
Pettitt, Stephen: Philharmonia Orchestra: A Record of Achievement, 1948-1985
Pettitt, Stephen (ed. Hunt): Philharmonia Orchestra: Discography 1945-1987
Playford, John: An Introduction to the Skill of Musick.
Porte, John: Sir Charles Villiers Stanford.
Quantz, Johann: Versuch einer Anweisung die Flöte traversiere zu spielen.
Rameau, Jean-Philippe: Code de Musique Pratique, ou Methodes.
Rameau, Jean-Philippe: Erreurs sur La Musique dans l'Encyclopédie
Rastall, Richard: The Notation of Western Music.
Rimbault, Edward: The Pianoforte, Its Origins, Progress, and Construction.
Rousseau, Jean Jacques: Dictionnaire de Musique
Rubinstein, Anton : Guide to the proper use of the Pianoforte Pedals.
Sainsbury, John S.: Dictionary of Musicians. (1825). (2 vols.)
Schumann, Clara & Brahms, Johannes: Letters 1853-1896. (2 vols.)
Serré de Rieux, Jean de : Les dons des Enfans de Latone
Simpson, Christopher: A Compendium of Practical Musick in Five Parts
Smyth, Ethel: Impressions That Remained. (2 vols.)
Spohr, Louis: Autobiography
Spohr, Louis: Grand Violin School
Tans'ur, William: A New Musical Grammar; or The Harmonical Spectator
Terry, Charles Sanford: Bach's Chorals – Parts 1, 2 and 3.
Terry, Charles Sanford: John Christian Bach
Terry, Charles Sanford: J.S. Bach's Original Hymn-Tunes - Congregational Use.
Terry, Charles Sanford: Four-Part Chorals of J.S. Bach. (German & English)
Terry, Charles Sanford: Joh. Seb. Bach, Cantata Texts, Sacred and Secular.
Terry, Charles Sanford: The Origins of the Family of Bach Musicians.
Tosi, Pierfrancesco: Opinioni de' Cantori Antichi, e Moderni
Tosi, Pierfrancesco: Observations on the Florid Song.
Tovey, Donald Francis: A Musician Talks, The Integrity of Music
Tovey, Donald Francis: A Musician Talks, Musical Textures
Tovey, Donald Francis: A Companion to "The Art of the Fugue" J.S. Bach
Tovey, Donald Francis: A Companion to Beethoven's Pianoforte Sonatas
Tovey, Donald Francis: Beethoven
Tovey, Donald Francis: Essays in Musical Analysis. (6 vols.).
Tovey, Donald Francis: The integrity of music
Tovey, Donald Francis: Musical Textures

Books published by Travis & Emery Music Bookshop:

Tovey, Donald Francis: Some English Symphonists
Tovey, Donald Francis: The Main Stream of Music.
Van der Straeten, Edmund: History of the Violoncello, The Viol da Gamba …
Van der Straeten, Edmund: History of the Violin, Its Ancestors… (2 vols.)
Walther, J. G. [Waltern]: Musicalisches Lexikon [Musikalisches Lexicon]
Wagner, Richard: Beethoven (Leipzig 1870)
Wagner, Richard: Lebens-Bericht (Leipzig 1884)
Wagner, Richard: The Musaic of the Future (Translated by E. Dannreuther).
Wyndham, Henry Saxe: The Annals of Covent Garden Theatre. (2 vols.)
Zwirn, Gerald: Stranded Stories From The Operas

Books Distributed by Travis & Emery Music Bookshop:

Herbert-Caesari, Edgar: The Alchemy of Voice

Music published by Travis & Emery Music Bookshop:

Bach, Johann Sebastian: Sacred Songs for SCTB, arranged by Franz Wullner.
Bax, Arnold: Symphony #5, Arranged for Piano Four Hands by Walter Emery
Beranger, Pierre Jean de: Musique Des Chansons de Beranger: Airs Notes ...
Bizet, Georges: Djamileh. Vocal Score.
Donizetti, Gaetano: Betly. Dramma Giocoso in Due Atti. Vocal Score.
Frescobaldi, Girolamo: D'Arie Musicali per Cantarsi. Primo & Secondo Libro.
Handel, Purcell, Boyce, Greene ... Calliope or English Harmony: Volume First.
Hopkins, Antony: Sonatine
Purcell, Henry et al: Harmonia Sacra … The First Book, (1726)
Purcell, Henry et al: Harmonia Sacra … Book II (1726)
Sullivan, Arthur Seymour: Ivanhoe. Vocal score.
Sullivan, Arthur Seymour: The Rose of Persia. Vocal Score.
Weckerlin, Jean-Baptiste: Chansons Populaires du Pays de France

Other Books, not on Music:

Anon: A Collection of Testimonies Concerning Several Ministers of the Gospel Amongst People called Quakers, Deceased. [Facsimile of 1760 edn.].
Sandeman-Allen, Arthur: Bee-keeping with Twenty hives.

Available from: Travis & Emery at 17 Cecil Court, London, UK.
(+44) (0) 20 7 240 2129. email on sales@travis-and-emery.com .

Discographies by John Hunt.

3 Italian Conductors and 7 Viennese Sopranos: 10 Discographies: Arturo Toscanini, Guido Cantelli, Carlo Maria Giulini, Elisabeth Schwarzkopf, Irmgard Seefried, Elisabeth Gruemmer, Sena Jurinac, Hilde Gueden, Lisa Della Casa, Rita Streich.
A Gallic Trio: 3 Discographies: Charles Muench, Paul Paray, Pierre Monteux.
A Notable Quartet: 4 Discographies: Gundula Janowitz, Christa Ludwig, Nicolai Gedda, Dietrich Fischer-Dieskau.
American Classics: The Discographies of Leonard Bernstein & Eugene Ormand
Antal Dorati 1906-1988: Discography and Concert Register.
Back From The Shadows: 4 Discographies: Willem Mengelberg, Dimitri Mitropoulos, Hermann Abendroth, Eduard Van Beinum.
Carlo Maria Giulini: Discography and Concert Register.
Columbia 33CX Label Discography.
Concert Hall Discography: Concert Hall Society and Concert Hall Record Club
Conductors On The Yellow Label: 8 Discographies: Fritz Lehmann, Ferdinand Leitner, Ferenc Fricsay, Eugen Jochum, Leopold Ludwig, Artur Rother, Franz Konwitschny, Igor Markevitch.
Dirigenten der DDR: Conductors of the German Democratic Republic
From Adam to Webern: the Recordings of von Karajan.
Frosh: Discography of the Richard Strauss Opera Die Frau ohne Schatten
Giants of the Keyboard: 6 Discographies: Wilhelm Kempff, Walter Gieseking, Edwin Fischer, Clara Haskil, Wilhelm Backhaus, Artur Schnabel.
Gramophone Stalwarts: 3 Separate Discographies: Bruno Walter, Erich Leinsdorf, Georg Solti.
Great Violinists: 3 Discographies: David Oistrakh, Wolfgang Schneiderhan, Arthur Grumiaux.
Hans Knappertsbusch: Kna: Concert Register and Discography of Hans Knappertsbusch, 1888-1965. Second Edition.
Her Master's Voice: Concert Register and Discography of Dame Elisabeth Schwarzkopf [Third Edition].
Hungarians in Exile: 3 Discographies: Fritz Reiner, Antal Dorati, George Szell.
Leopold Stokowski (1882-1977): Discography and Concert Register
Leopold Stokowski: Discography and Concert Listing.
Leopold Stokowski: Second Edition of the Discography.
Makers of the Philharmonia: 11 Discographies Alceo Galliera, Walter Susskind, Paul Kletzki, Nicolai Malko, Issay Dobrowen, Lovro Von Matacic, Efrem Kurtz, Otto Ackermann, Anatole Fistoulari, George Weldon, Robert Irving.
Metropolitan Sopranos: 4 Discographies: Rosa Ponselle, Eleanor Steber, Zinka Milanov, Leontyne Price.
Mezzo and Contraltos: 5 Discographies: Janet Baker, Margarete Klose, Kathleen Ferrier, Giulietta Simionato, Elisabeth Hoengen.

Mid-Century Conductors and More Viennese Singers: 10 Discographies: Karl Boehm, Victor De Sabata, Hans Knappertsbusch, Tullio Serafin, Clemens Krauss, Anton Dermota, Leonie Rysanek, Eberhard Waechter, Maria Reining, Erich Kunz.
More 20th Century Conductors: 7 Discographies: Eugen Jochum, Ferenc Fricsay, Carl Schuricht, Felix Weingartner, Josef Krips, Otto Klemperer, Erich Kleiber.
More Giants of the Keyboard: 5 Discographies: Claudio Arrau, Gyorgy Cziffra, Vladimir Horowitz, Dinu Lipatti, Artur Rubinstein.
More Musical Knights: 4 Discographies: Hamilton Harty, Charles Mackerras, Simon Rattle, John Pritchard.
Musical Knights: 6 Discographies: Henry Wood, Thomas Beecham, Adrian Boult, John Barbirolli, Reginald Goodall, Malcolm Sargent.
Philharmonic Autocrat 1: Discography of: Herbert Von Karajan [Third Edition]
Philharmonic Autocrat 2: Concert Register of Herbert Von Karajan Second Ed.
Philips Minigroove: Second Extended Version of the European Discography.
Pianists For The Connoisseur: 6 Discographies: Arturo Benedetti Michelangeli, Alfred Cortot, Alexis Weissenberg, Clifford Curzon, Solomon, Elly Ney.
Sächsische Staatskapelle Dresden: Complete Discography.
Singers of the Third Reich: 5 Discographies: Helge Roswaenge, Tiana Lemnitz, Franz Voelker, Maria Mueller, Max Lorenz.
Singers on the Yellow Label: 7 Discographies: Maria Stader, Elfriede Troetschel, Annelies Kupper, Wolfgang Windgassen, Ernst Haefliger, Josef Greindl, Kim Borg
Six Wagnerian Sopranos: 6 Discographies: Frieda Leider, Kirsten Flagstad, Astrid Varnay, Martha Moedl, Birgit Nilsson, Gwyneth Jones.
Sviatoslav Richter: Pianist of the Century: Discography.
Teachers and Pupils: 7 Discographies: Elisabeth Schwarzkopf, Maria Ivoguen, Maria Cebotari, Meta Seinemeyer, Ljuba Welitsch, Rita Streich, Erna Berger
Tenors in a Lyric Tradition: 3 Discographies: Peter Anders, Walther Ludwig, Fritz Wunderlich.
The Art of the Diva: 3 Discographies: Claudia Muzio, Maria Callas, Magda Olivero.
The Furtwaengler Sound Sixth Edition: Discography and Concert Listing.
The Great Dictators: 3 Discographies: Evgeny Mravinsky, Artur Rodzinski, Sergiu Celibidache.
The Lyric Baritone: 5 Discographies: Hans Reinmar, Gerhard Huesch, Josef Metternich, Hermann Uhde, Eberhard Waechter.
The Post-War German Tradition: 5 Discographies: Rudolf Kempe, Joseph Keilberth, Wolfgang Sawallisch, Rafael Kubelik, Andre Cluytens.
Wagner Im Festspielhaus: Discography of the Bayreuth Festival.
Wiener Philharmoniker 1 - Vienna Philharmonic and Vienna State Opera Orchestras: Discography Part 1 1905-1954.
Wiener Philharmoniker 2 - Vienna Philharmonic and Vienna State Opera Orchestras: Discography Part 2 1954-1989.

Available from: Travis & Emery at 17 Cecil Court, London, UK.
(+44) (0) 20 7 240 2129. email on sales@travis-and-emery.com .

© Travis & Emery 2012

www.ingramcontent.com/pod-product-compliance
Lightning Source LLC
Chambersburg PA
CBHW071842230426
43671CB00012B/2042